Advance Reviews for *SSL & TLS Essentials*

"A complete and useful guide for network administrators and programmers."

Tim Dierks
Chief Technology Officer
Certicom
co-author of RFC 2246, the TLS Standard

"An excellent companion for all professionals working on Internet and Web related businesses. Core security procedures and protocols are presented in very clear terms, avoiding the usual impenetrable technical language common in this field. Security protocols, cryptography, certificates and the associated message exchanges are explained in simple narrative, associated by excellent graphics and tables. Practical use not only to Web authors and people doing business on the Web, but also to a large population of network and telecommunication engineers, managers and executives."

Henry Sinnreich
Distinguished Technical Member
MCI WorldCom Engineering

"A straightforward explanation of one of the most important developments necessary for the commercialization of the Internet. Thomas does it again by using the same easy-to-understand style that made his previous book, *IPng and the TCP/IP Protocols*, a cornerstone Internet Protocol reference."

Michael A. Ramalho, Ph.D.
Cisco Systems
Rutgers University CAIP Fellow

"A concise and complete guide to these important Internet protocols. The appendix on ASN.1 is one of the best explanations I've read of this complex data structure definition language, and will be helpful in understanding a number of other standards in addition to X.509 certificates. A good choice for computer professionals seeking an introduction before evaluating an SSL implementation or beginning one of their own."

Toby Nixon
Windows Networking and Embedded Products
Microsoft Corporation

More Advance Reviews

"A good overview of the SSL protocol for both a beginner and a security professional. The first book that provides extensive knowledge of the SSL protocol, with all information essential for understanding SSL and the SSL messages. A five star rating."

Bernd Adams and Tobias Martin
Deutsche Telekom

"An easy to follow book that allows the reader to understand the need for and the application of the current standard security system in the world of e-commerce. It not only explains in a concise and clear way the technical aspects at a sufficient level for an uninformed reader to follow, but also provides additional technical detail on the operation of SSL for those who wish to gain a deeper understanding. This is a book that should appeal to a wide range of readers and would be a valuable addition to the bookshelf of anyone involved in Web based commerce."

Tony Avoner
Principal Engineer – Standards
Cable & Wireless Communications

"A good read both as an introduction and as a work of reference. Thomas writes well and explains the subject in the clearest way that I have seen."

Paul Sijben
Lucent Technologies

"Great writing. It's rare to have clear and simple descriptions of complex protocols. The book contains all the figures and illustrations that should have been in the specification. It provides a clear introduction to the most widely deployed security technology in the Internet."

Paul Lambert
Certicom
former co-chair of IETF IPSEC Working Group

SSL & TLS Essentials

Securing the Web

SSL & TLS Essentials

Securing the Web

Stephen A. Thomas

Wiley Computer Publishing
John Wiley & Sons, Inc.
New York • Chichester • Weinheim • Brisbane • Singapore • Toronto

Publisher: Robert Ipsen
Editor: Marjorie Spencer
Assistant Editor: Margaret Hendrey
Text Design & Composition: Stephen Thomas

Published by John Wiley & Sons, Inc.

Published simultaneously in Canada.

Library of Congress Cataloging-in-Publication Data:

Thomas, Stephen A., 1962-
    SSL and TLS essentials : securing the Web / Stephen A. Thomas.
       p. cm.
    Includes index.
    ISBN 0-471-38354-6 (pbk./cd-rom : alk. paper)
    1. Computer networks--Security measures. 2. World Wide Web--Security measures. 3. Computer network protocols. I. Title.
    TK5105.59 .T49 2000
    005.8--dc21   99-058910

Printed in the United States of America.

10 9 8 7 6 5 4 3 2 1

For Kelsie,
Zookeeper of Mango the Flamingo.

Contents

1

Introduction

Today alone, Dell Computer will sell more than $18 million worth of computer equipment through the Internet. In 1999, nine million Americans traded stocks online, accounting for one-third of all retail stock trades. And more than 200,000 Web sites worldwide (including sites belonging to 98 of the Fortune 100) can accept e-commerce transactions. Commercial use of the Web continues to grow at an astonishing pace, and securing Web transactions has become increasingly critical to businesses, organizations, and individual users.

Fortunately, an extremely effective and widely deployed communications protocol provides exactly that security. It is the Secure Sockets Layer protocol, more commonly known simply as SSL. The SSL protocol—along with its successor, the Transport Layer Security (TLS) protocol—is the subject of this book.

This chapter introduces SSL and TLS, and provides the essential context for both. It begins with a very brief look at Web security and electronic commerce, focusing on the issues that led to the creation of SSL. The next section follows up with a quick history of SSL and its transformation into TLS. The relationship of SSL to other network security technologies is the subject of the third section. The forth section, "Protocol Limitations," is an important one. Especially with security technologies, it is critical to understand what they *cannot* do. The chapter closes with an overview of the rest of this book.

1.1 Web Security and Electronic Commerce

Know the enemy. Sun Tzu could not have offered any advice more appropriate to security professionals. Specific security services are necessarily effective against only specific threats; they may be completely inappropriate for other security threats. To understand SSL, therefore, it is essential to understand the environment for which it has been designed.

Even though SSL is a flexible protocol that is finding use in many different applications, the original motivation for its development was the Internet. The protocol's designers needed to secure electronic commerce and other Web transactions. That environment is certainly perilous enough. Consider, for example, what happens when a user in Berlin places an online order from a Web site in San Jose, California. Table 1-1 lists the systems through which the user's messages might pass.

Table 1-1 Internet Systems in Path from Berlin to San Jose

Step	IP Address	System Name (if known)
1	212.211.70.7	
2	212.211.70.254	
3	195.232.91.66	fra-ppp2-fas1-0-0.wan.wcom.net
4	212.211.30.29	
5	206.175.73.45	hil-border1-atm4-0-2.wan.wcom.net
6	205.156.223.41	dub-border1-hss2-0.wan.wcom.net
7	204.70.98.101	borderx1-hssi2-0.northroyalton.cw.net
8	204.70.98.49	core2-fddi-0.northroyalton.cw.net
9	204.70.9.138	corerouter1.westorange.cw.net
10	204.70.4.101	core5.westorange.cw.net
11	204.70.10.230	sprint4-nap.westorange.cw.net
12	192.157.69.85	sprint-nap.home.net
13	24.7.72.113	c1-pos9-1.cmdnnj1.home.net
14	24.7.67.153	c1-pos6-2.clevoh1.home.net
15	24.7.64.173	c1-pos3-0.chcgil1.home.net
16	24.7.64.141	c1-pos1-0.omahne1.home.net

Step	IP Address	System Name (if known)
17	24.7.66.173	c1-pos8-3.lnmtco1.home.net
18	24.7.64.57	c1-pos1-0.slkcut1.home.net
19	24.7.66.77	c1-pos5-3.snjsca1.home.net
20	24.7.72.18	bb1-pos6-0-0.rdc1.sfba.home.net
21	172.16.6.194	
22	10.252.84.3	
23	10.252.10.150	
24	209.219.157.152	www.sj-downtown.com

Figure 1-1 highlights the fact that messages containing the user's information, including sensitive information such as credit card numbers, may travel a complex path from Germany to California, crossing through many countries, over various networks, and on many different facilities. Some of those facilities are likely to belong to private enterprises, many of which are not subject to any regulation or other laws governing the privacy of the information they transport.

Neither the user nor the Web server has any control over the path their messages take, nor can they control who examines the message contents along the route. From a security standpoint, it's as if the user wrote her credit card number on a postcard and then delivered

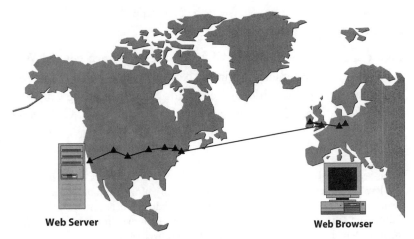

Web Server   **Web Browser**

Figure 1-1 Messages travel complex paths through the Internet.

the postcard as a message in a bottle. The user has no control over how the message reaches its destination, and anyone along the way can easily read its contents. Electronic commerce cannot thrive in such an insecure environment; sensitive information must be kept confidential as it traverses the Internet.

Eavesdropping isn't the only security threat to Web users. It is theoretically possible to divert Web messages to a counterfeit Web site. Such a counterfeit site could provide false information, collect data such as credit card numbers with impunity, or create other mischief.[1] The Internet needs a way to assure users of a Web site's true identity; likewise, many Web sites need to verify the identity of their users.

A final security challenge facing Web users is message integrity. A user placing an online stock trade certainly wouldn't want his instructions garbled in such a way as to change "Sell when the price reaches $200" to "Sell when the price reaches $20." The missing zero can make a significant difference in the user's fortunes.

1.2 History of SSL and TLS

Fortunately, engineers were thinking about these security issues from the Web's beginnings. Netscape Communications began considering Web security while developing its very first Web browser. To address the concerns of the previous section, Netscape designed the Secure Sockets Layer protocol.

Figure 1-2 shows the evolution of ssl in the context of general Web development. The timeline begins in November 1993, with the release of Mosaic 1.0 by the National Center for Supercomputing Applications (ncsa). Mosaic was the first popular Web browser. Only eight months later, Netscape Communications completed the design for

---

[1] This security threat isn't unique to the Web. In *Computer-Related Risks* (Addison-Wesley, 1995), Peter G. Neumann recounts the story of two criminals who set up a bogus atm in a Connecticut mall. The machine didn't dispense much cash, but it did capture the account number and pin of unsuspecting victims. The crooks then fabricated phony atm cards and allegedly withdrew over $100 000.

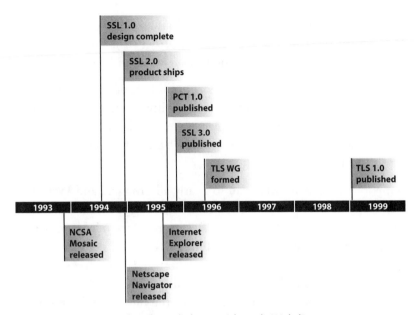

Figure 1-2 SSL was developed along with early Web browsers.

SSL version 1.0; five months after that, Netscape shipped the first product with support for SSL version 2.0—Netscape Navigator.

Other milestones in the timeline include the publication of version 1.0 of the Private Communication Technology (PCT) specification. Microsoft developed PCT as a minor enhancement to SSL version 2.0. It addressed some of the weaknesses of SSL 2.0, and many of its ideas were later incorporated into SSL version 3.0.

The later events on the timeline represent a shift in focus for the SSL standard. Netscape Communications developed the first three versions of SSL with significant assistance from the Web community. Although SSL's development was open, and Netscape encouraged others in the industry to participate, the protocol technically belonged to Netscape. (Indeed, Netscape has been granted a U.S. patent for SSL.) Beginning in May 1996, however, SSL development became the responsibility of an international standards organization—the Internet Engineering Task Force (IETF). The IETF develops many of the protocol standards for the Internet, including, for example, TCP and IP.

To avoid the appearance of bias toward any particular company, the IETF renamed SSL to *Transport Layer Security* (TLS). The final version of the first official TLS specification was released in January 1999.

Despite the change of names, TLS is nothing more than a new version of SSL. In fact, there are far fewer differences between TLS 1.0 and SSL 3.0 than there are between SSL 3.0 and SSL 2.0. Section 5.4 details the differences between SSL and TLS, but check the sidebars for more information.

Support for SSL is now built in to nearly all browsers and Web servers. For users of Netscape Navigator or Microsoft's Internet Explorer, SSL operates nearly transparently. Observant users might notice the "https:" prefix for an SSL-secured URL, or they may see a small icon that each browser displays when SSL is in use. (Figure 1-3 shows the padlock symbol that Internet Explorer displays in the bottom status bar; Navigator shows a similar icon.) For the most part, however, SSL simply works, safely providing confidentiality, authentication, and message integrity to its Web users.

Today's popular Web servers also include support for SSL. It's usually a simple task to enable SSL in the server. As we'll see, though, to support secure Web browsing, a Web server must do more than simply enable the SSL protocol. The server must also obtain a public key certificate from an organization that Web browsers trust. For users on the public Internet, those organizations are generally public certificate authorities. Popular certificate authorities include AT&T Certificate Services, GTE CyberTrust, KeyWitness International, Microsoft, Thawte Consulting, and VeriSign. The next chapter includes further discussions of certificate authorities (primarily in section 2.3.2), and appendix A provides details on public key certificates.

SSL vs. TLS

Because SSL is more widely used and much better known than TLS, the main text of this book describes SSL rather than TLS. The differences between the two are very minor, however. Sidebars such as this one will note all those differences.

1.3 Approaches to Network Security

The Secure Sockets Layer protocol provides effective security for Web transactions, but it is not the only possible approach. The Internet architecture relies on layers of protocols, each building on the services of those below it. Many of these different protocol layers can

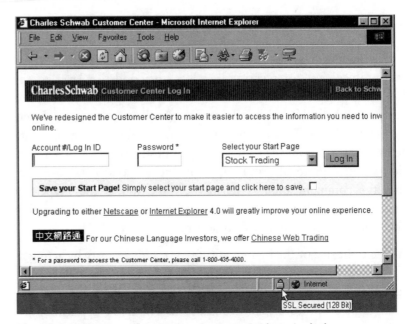

Figure 1-3 Web browsers such as Internet Explorer include SSL.

support security services, though each has its own advantages and disadvantages. As we'll see in this section, the designers of SSL chose to create an entirely new protocol layer for security. It is also possible to include security services in the application protocol or to add them to a core networking protocol. As another alternative, applications can rely on parallel protocols for some security services. All of these options have been considered for securing Web transactions, and actual protocols exist for each alternative. Table 1-2 summarizes the advantages of each approach, and this section considers each of the possible approaches in more detail.

Table 1-2 Different Approaches to Network Security

Protocol Architecture	Example	A	B	C	D	E
Separate Protocol Layer	SSL	●	●	○	○	●
Application Layer	S-HTTP	●	○	●	○	●
Integrated with Core	IPSEC	●	●	○	●	○
Parallel Protocol	Kerberos	○	●	○	○	●

Benefits: A – Full Security B – Multiple Applications C – Tailored Services
D – Transparent to Application E – Easy to Deploy

1.3.1 Separate Security Protocol

The designers of the Secure Sockets Layer decided to create a separate protocol just for security. In effect, they added a layer to the Internet's protocol architecture. The left side of figure 1-4 shows the key protocols for Web communications. At the bottom is the Internet Protocol (IP). This protocol is responsible for routing messages across networks from their source to their destination. The Transmission Control Protocol (TCP) builds on the services of IP to ensure that the communication is reliable. At the top is the Hypertext Transfer Protocol; HTTP understands the details of the interaction between Web browsers and Web servers.

As the right side of the figure indicates, SSL adds security by acting as a separate security protocol, inserting itself between the HTTP application and TCP. By acting as a new protocol, SSL requires very few changes in the protocols above and below. The HTTP application interfaces with SSL nearly the same way it would with TCP in the absence of security. And, as far as TCP is concerned, SSL is just another application using its services.

In addition to requiring minimal changes to existing implementations, this approach has another significant benefit: It allows SSL to support applications other than HTTP. The main motivation behind the development of SSL was Web security, but, as figure 1-5 shows, SSL

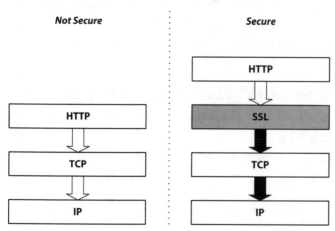

Figure 1-4 SSL is a separate protocol layer just for security.

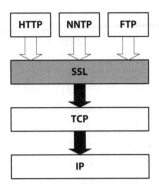

Figure 1-5 SSL can add security to applications other than HTTP.

is also used to add security to other Internet applications, including those of the Net News Transfer Protocol (NNTP) and the File Transfer Protocol (FTP).

1.3.2 Application-Specific Security

Although the designers of SSL chose a different strategy, it is also possible to add security services directly in an application protocol. Indeed, standard HTTP does include some extremely rudimentary security features; however, those security features don't provide adequate protection for real electronic commerce. At about the same time Netscape was designing SSL, another group of protocol designers was working on an enhancement to HTTP known as Secure HTTP. Figure 1-6 shows the resulting protocol architecture. The Secure HTTP standard has been published by the IETF as an experimental

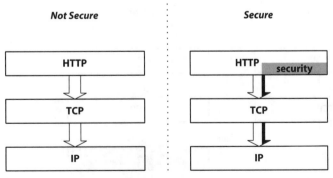

Figure 1-6 Security can be added directly within an application protocol.

protocol, and a few products support it. It never caught on to the same degree as SSL, however, and oday it is rare to find Secure HTTP anywhere on the Internet.

One of the disadvantages of adding security to a specific application is that the security services are available only to that particular application. Unlike SSL, for example, it is not possible to secure NNTP, FTP, or other application protocols with Secure HTTP. Another disadvantage of this approach is that it ties the security services tightly to the application. Every time the application protocol changes, the security implications must be carefully considered, and, frequently, the security functions of the protocol must be modified as well. A separate protocol like SSL isolates security services from the application protocol, allowing each to concentrate on solving its own problems most effectively.

1.3.3   Security within Core Protocols

The separate protocol approach of SSL can be taken one step further if security services are added directly to a core networking protocol. That is exactly the approach of the IP security (IPSEC) architecture; full security services become an optional part of the Internet Protocol itself. Figure 1-7 illustrates the IPSEC architecture.

The IPSEC architecture has many of the same advantages as SSL. It is independent of the application protocol, so any application may use it. In most cases, the application does not need to change at all to

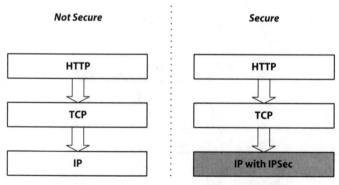

Figure 1-7 IPSEC adds security to a core network protocol.

take advantage of IPSEC. In fact, it may even be completely unaware that IPSEC is involved at all. This feature does create its own challenges, however, as IPSEC must be sufficiently flexible to support all applications. This complexity may be a big factor in the delays in development and deployment of IPSEC.

Another concern with the IPSEC approach is that it provides too much isolation between the application and security services. At least in its simplest implementations, IPSEC tends to assume that secure requirements are a function of a particular system, and that all applications within that system need the same security services. The SSL approach provides isolation between applications and security, but it allows some interaction between the two. The internal behavior of an application such as HTTP need not change when security is added, but the application typically has to make the decision to use SSL or not. Such interaction makes it easier for each application to direct the security services most appropriate to its needs.

Despite these drawbacks, IPSEC adds powerful new security tools to the Internet, and it will undoubtedly see widespread deployment. The SSL protocol, however, has significant benefits as well, and its deployment is also expected to grow substantially in the future.

1.3.4 Parallel Security Protocol

There is yet a fourth approach to adding security services to an application—a parallel security protocol. The most popular example of this strategy is the Kerberos protocol developed by the Massachusetts Institute of Technology. Researchers developed Kerberos to provide authentication and access control for resources in a distributed environment. The Kerberos protocol acts as a toolkit that other protocols can use for those security services. A remote login protocol such as Telnet, for example, can use Kerberos to securely identify its user.

In the very early days of Web browser development, some effort was made to incorporate Kerberos support within HTTP. Figure 1-8 shows the resulting architecture. This work was never completed, though. Instead, there have been recent efforts to combine Kerberos with TLS. In such applications, Kerberos provides a trusted key exchange

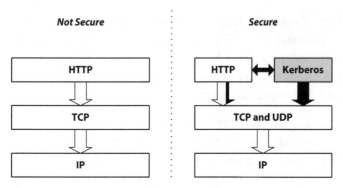

Figure 1-8 Kerberos supplements application protocols.

mechanism for Transport Layer Security. Note, though, that Kerberos alone is not a complete security solution. It does not have access to the actual information exchanged by the communicating parties. Without that access, Kerberos cannot provide encryption and decryption services.

1.4 Protocol Limitations

The SSL protocol, like any technology, has its limitations. And because SSL provides security services, it is especially important to understand its limits. After all, a false sense of security may be worse than no security. The limitations of SSL fall generally into three categories. First are fundamental constraints of the SSL protocol itself. These are a consequence of the design of SSL and its intended application. The SSL protocol also inherits some weaknesses from the tools its uses, namely encryption and signature algorithms. If these algorithms have weaknesses, SSL generally cannot rehabilitate them. Finally, the environments in which SSL is deployed have their own shortcomings and limitations, some of which SSL is helpless to address.

1.4.1 Fundamental Protocol Limitations

Though its design includes considerations for many different applications, SSL is definitely focused on securing Web transactions. Some of its characteristics reflect that concentration. For example, SSL requires a reliable transport protocol such as TCP. That is a completely reasonable requirement in the world of Web transactions, because the Hypertext Transfer Protocol itself requires TCP. The decision means, however, that SSL cannot operate using a connectionless transport protocol like UDP.[2] With this significant exception, Web transactions are representative of general network computing environments. The SSL protocol, therefore, can effectively accommodate most common applications quite well. Indeed, SSL is in use today for securing various applications, including file transfer, network news reading, and remote login.

Another role that SSL fails to fill is support for a particular security service known as *non-repudiation*. Non-repudiation associates the digital equivalent of a signature with data, and when used properly, it prevents the party that creates and "signs" data from successfully denying that after the fact. The SSL protocol does not provide non-repudiation services, so SSL alone would not be appropriate for an application that required it.

1.4.2 Tool Limitations

The Secure Sockets Layer is simply a communication protocol, and any SSL implementation will rely on other components for many functions, including the cryptographic algorithms. These algorithms are the mathematical tools that actually perform tasks such as encryption and decryption. No SSL implementation can be any stronger than the cryptographic tools on which it is based.

As of this writing, SSL itself has no known significant weaknesses. Some common cryptographic algorithms, however, have been successfully attacked, at least in the context of academics or other research. (There are no publicly acknowledged cases of anyone

---

[2] Although neither SSL nor TLS can use UDP, the Wireless Application Forum, an industry group developing standards for Internet access protocols for wireless devices such as mobile phones, has created a variation of TLS known as Wireless TLS (WTLS), which can support UDP. More information is available at http://www.wapforum.org.

exploiting these theoretical weaknesses in a commercial context.) Appendix B describes the publicly reported attacks in more detail, but, in general, SSL implementations must consider not only the security of SSL, but also that of the cryptographic services on which it is built.

1.4.3   Environmental Limitations

A network protocol alone can only provide security for information as it transits a network. No network protocol protects data before it is sent or after it arrives at its destination. This is the only known weakness in Web security that has been successfully exploited in an actual commercial setting. Unfortunately, it has been exploited more than once.[3]

Security in any computer network, whether the public Internet or private facilities, is a function of all the elements that make up that network. It depends on the network security protocols, the computer systems that use those protocols, and the human beings who use those computers. No network security protocol can protect against the confidential printout carelessly left on a cafeteria table.

The Secure Sockets Layer protocol is a strong and effective security tool, but it is only a single tool. True security requires many such tools, and a comprehensive plan to employ them.

1.5   Organization of This Book

Four more chapters and two appendices make up the rest of this book. Chapter 2 looks at some of the essential principles of cryptography and cryptographic algorithms. Although, strictly speaking, these algorithms are not part of the SSL protocol, a good bit of the protocol's design depends on general cryptographic principles. Without getting too deep into the mathematics of cryptography, chapter 2

---

[3] See, for example, the 8 November 1996 edition of *The Wall Street Journal* (page B6) or the 11 July 1997 issue of *The San Francisco Chronicle* (page C3).

examines those essential principles. Chapter 3 begins the examination of SSL in earnest. It describes the SSL protocol in operation. It discusses the contents of SSL messages, but only in general terms. The chapter explains *what* SSL does without getting bogged down in the details of *how* it does it. Chapter 4, on the other hand, focuses exclusively on those details. It documents the format of all SSL messages, as well as the cryptographic calculations SSL uses to construct them. Chapter 5 provides additional details about SSL. It describes how the current version of SSL operates with previous SSL versions, and how Netscape and Microsoft have each augmented SSL with techniques that promote strong encryption worldwide, while adhering to United States export restrictions. This chapter also provides complete coverage of Transport Layer Security, detailing all the differences between TLS and SSL.

Appendix A provides additional details on public key certificates. These certificates, which conform to the x.509 standard, are critical to the operation of SSL, even though they are not part of the protocol itself. The appendix includes a brief introduction to Abstract Syntax Notation One, the language that the x.509 standard uses to document certificates. Appendix B presents a security checklist for SSL. It includes a list of good practices for the development of SSL implementations, and defenses against all known attacks against SSL-secured systems.

2

Basic Cryptography

The Web may be a relatively new way to communicate, but securing the Web relies on the same principles that have secured other communications media for thousands of years. In fact, the digital nature of the Web actually makes it easier to apply these techniques. In addition, systems on the Web can take advantage of new and powerful security technology. This chapter takes a brief look at the important principles that govern communications security.

The scientific discipline that studies communications security is *cryptography*, and several concepts from modern cryptography are indispensable to the Secure Sockets Layer protocol. The first of the following three sections describes the uses of cryptography. The next section looks in more detail at two particular types of cryptography—secret key cryptography and public key cryptography. As the names imply, *keys* are an important part of both types, and this chapter concludes by discussing the management of these keys. Key management plays a critical role in the operation of SSL.

As the following text implies, cryptography relies heavily on a mathematical foundation. But understanding the mathematics of cryptography is not essential for understanding SSL. For that reason, this chapter contains very little mathematics. Readers who are interested in a more thorough understanding of cryptography are invited to consult the texts described in the References section of this book.

2.1 Using Cryptography

The word cryptography is derived from the Greek for "secret writing." The task of keeping information secret is probably the one most often associated with cryptography. Indeed, protecting secret information is an important mission for cryptographers, but, as this section shows, cryptography has other uses as well. Two that are particularly important to SSL are proving identity and verifying information. Table 2-1 summarizes the main topics of this section.

Table 2-1 Important Uses of Cryptography

Use	Service	Protects Against
Keeping secrets	Confidentiality	Eavesdropping
Proving identity	Authentication	Forgery and masquerade
Verifying information	Message integrity	Alteration

2.1.1 Keeping Secrets

To continue with a convention that has become almost universal in cryptography texts, consider the dilemma facing Alice and Bob in figure 2-1. Alice needs to send Bob some important information. The

Figure 2-1 Cryptography can protect information from eavesdroppers.

information is extremely confidential, and it is important that no one other than Bob receive it. If, as in this example, the only way that Alice can communicate with Bob is by postcard, how can she send him the information without exposing it to mail carriers, snooping neighbors, or anyone else that happens to see the vital postcard?

Cryptography gives Alice and Bob the means to protect their exchange. Before sending the postcard, Alice uses a secret code, or *cipher*, that only she and Bob understand. The cipher scrambles the information, rendering it unintelligible to parties such as Charles that do not know the secret code. Bob, however, knows the secret code and can decipher the necessary information.

2.1.2 Proving Identity

Now consider the situation in figure 2-2. Bob receives a postcard with important information, purportedly from Alice. But how does he know that the postcard really came from Alice? Might Charles have forged the card to make it appear as if from Alice? Again, cryptography provides a solution.

Figure 2-2 Cryptography can help verify a sender's identity.

Through the use of cryptography, Alice can attach special information, such as a secret phrase, to the postcard. This secret phrase is information that only she and Bob know. Since Charles does not know the secret phrase, he will not be able to attach it to any forgery. Now all Bob has to do is look for the secret phrase. If it is present, then the postcard is genuine; if it is absent, he should be suspicious.

2.1.3   Verifying Information

Proving identity is one thing, but suppose Charles is able to intercept a genuine message to Bob from Alice. Charles could then modify the message and forward the altered message on to Bob, as in figure 2-3. Charles's changes might alter the meaning of the message significantly, yet not destroy the secret phrase that "proves" Alice was the sender. To protect against this kind of behavior, there must be a way to not only verify the identity of the message source, but also to ensure that the message contents have not been altered in any way. Again, cryptography offers a solution.

To validate the information on her postcard, Alice can use a special type of cryptographic function known as a *hash function*. A hash function creates a special mathematical summary of information. If the information is modified and the hash function recalculated, a different summary will result. To prevent Charles from successfully tampering with her postcard, Alice calculates the hash function for the information on the card, plus a secret value only she and Bob

Figure 2-3 Cryptography can ensure information has not been altered.

know. She then adds the resulting summary to the postcard. When Bob receives the card, he can also calculate the hash function. If his summary matches that on the card, the information is valid.

Cryptographic hash functions resemble checksums or cyclic redundancy check (CRC) codes that are common error detection mechanisms for traditional communication protocols. There is an important difference, though. Checksums and CRC codes are designed to detect accidental alterations, such as might occur on an unreliable transmission medium. Cryptographic hashes, on the other hand, are optimized to detect deliberate alterations. Because they assume the malicious attacker has full knowledge of the algorithm, and can thus exploit any weakness, effective hash functions are considerably harder to devise than standard error detection algorithms.

Two particular hash functions are essential to SSL implementations. The first is Message Digest 5 (MD5), devised by Ron Rivest. The other important hash function is the Secure Hash Algorithm (SHA), proposed by the U.S. National Institute of Science and Technology. Both will make their appearance in chapters 4 and 5 when we look at the details of the SSL and TLS specifications.

2.2 Types of Cryptography

As even the preceding brief introduction makes clear, one essential element of cryptography is the use of secret codes that are shared only by the communicating parties. Whether it's keeping secrets, proving identity, or verifying information, Alice and Bob must know some secret information that Charles does not. Cryptographers call that information a *key*.

Cryptographic techniques fall into two classifications, depending on the type of keys they use: *secret key cryptography* and *public key cryptography*. The following subsections describe each separately, then discuss how practical implementations often use a combination of the two approaches.

2.2.1 Secret Key Cryptography

With secret key cryptography, both parties know the same information—the key—and both endeavor to keep that key secret from everyone else. This is how most people think of cryptography in general, and, for nearly all of the several-thousand-year history of secret codes, it was the only form of cryptography known. The critical aspect of secret key cryptography is that both parties know the same secret information. For this reason, it has the technical name *symmetric encryption*.

Encryption algorithms, or *ciphers*, based on secret key techniques are usually just mathematical transformations on the data to be encrypted, combined with the secret key itself. The approach resembles a carnival shell game, with the secret key serving as the initial location of the pea. Bits are swapped around and combined with each other in very complicated ways, and yet the various transformations can readily be undone, provided one knows the key. As a hint of the complexities involved, Figure 2-4 illustrates one of the more common encryption algorithms. The figure also introduces two common cryptographic terms—*plaintext*, information before encryption, and *ciphertext*, information in its encrypted form. Plaintext is vulnerable to attackers; ciphertext, at least in theory, is not.

An important quality that determines the effectiveness of a cipher is the size of the secret key. The larger the key, the more difficult it is to break the code. To understand why this is the case, consider an algorithm with an extremely small key size: 2 bits. In this example, the algorithm itself really wouldn't matter. After all, with 2 bits there are only four possible keys. An attacker who obtained encrypted data could simply try all four possibilities.

Cryptographers also characterize symmetric encryption algorithms according to how they process input data. Ciphers may be either *stream ciphers* or *block ciphers*. Stream ciphers process input data a byte at a time, and can accept any size of input for encryption. Block ciphers, in contrast, operate only on fixed-sized blocks of data—typically 8 bytes in size. Block ciphers are require less computation resources, and they are generally slightly less vulnerable to attack

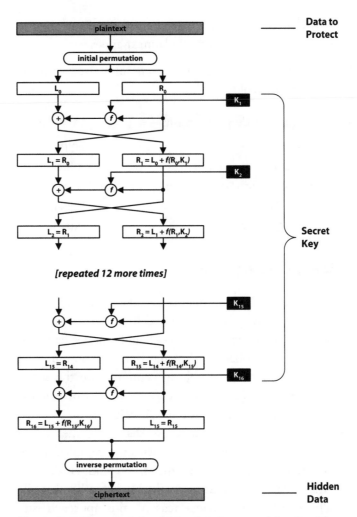

Figure 2-4 The DES cipher hides data by scrambling it with a secret key.

(and, thus, are by far the more common type). They are, however, slightly less convenient to use. The input data itself is the source of the inconvenience; it is rarely the same size as the cipher's block. Encrypting data using a block cipher requires breaking the data into blocks, and, if the last block doesn't contain exactly the right amount of data, adding dummy data, known as *padding*, to fill it out.

Block ciphers also usually require an *initialization vector* of dummy data to begin the encryption process. The initialization vector primes the algorithm with irrelevant information, enabling the cipher to build up to full strength before the actual plaintext appears.

Table 2-2 lists the symmetric ciphers most commonly used with the Secure Sockets Layer protocol.

Table 2-2 Symmetric Encryption Algorithms

Abbreviation	Algorithm	Type
DES	Data Encryption Standard	Block
3DES	Triple-Strength Data Encryption Standard	Block
RC2	Rivest Cipher 2	Block
RC4	Rivest Cipher 4	Stream

2.2.2 Public Key Cryptography

Most of the difficulties with traditional secret key cryptography are caused by the keys themselves. Both Alice and Bob need to have the same secret key, but under no circumstances should Charles have this key as well. That implies that before Alice and Bob can communicate information securely, they must be able to communicate the secret key securely. The problem mimics the classic chicken-or-egg dilemma. After all, if there's a secure way for Alice and Bob to communicate the secret key, why can't they use that same method to communicate the information, and dispense with the complexities of cryptography altogether? (In some situations, such as cloak-and-dagger spying, the two parties can agree on the key beforehand, while they're physically together; for obvious reasons, this approach isn't practical for situations in which the parties never meet face-to-face, such as Web-based commerce.)

A relatively new development in cryptography has eliminated the key distribution impasse and has made technology such as SSL and e-commerce possible. That development is *public key cryptography*. Public key cryptography or, more technically, *asymmetric encryption*, actually has each of the two parties use separate keys—one for encryption and a different one for decryption. The critical aspect of public key cryptography is that only one of these two keys needs to be kept secret. The other key, the *public key*, need not be secret at all.

Although it seems a bit like magic, this has a solid mathematical basis. Fundamentally, asymmetric encryption is based on mathematical problems that are mush easier to generate than they are to solve. As an example, anyone with a pocket calculator can compute the product of 113 and 293 and get the correct answer of 33 109. It is much more difficult, however, to use the same pocket calculator to work a similar problem in reverse. Which two whole numbers, when multiplied together, yield the product 29 213?[1]

Figure 2-5 shows how public key encryption can work. When Bob wants Alice to send him information securely, he generates two keys.

1 Create keys.

2 Publish public key.

3 Encipher with public key.

5 Decipher with private key.

4 Send encrypted message.

Alice   Bob

Figure 2-5 Public key cryptography uses published keys to encrypt data.

---

[1] The answer, for the insatiably curious, is 131 and 223.

One is the *private key*, which Bob keeps completely to himself. Conversely, Bob advertises the *public key*, conceptually even by publishing it in a newspaper. Alice reads the newspaper to find out the public key, then uses it to encrypt the information. When Bob receives Alice's postcard, his private key enables him to decipher the message. Since only Bob has his private key, only Bob can successfully decrypt the information. Even Alice would be unable to do so.

Some public key encryption algorithms, notably the Rivest Shamir Adleman (RSA) algorithm commonly used with SSL, also work in reverse. Information encrypted with a private key can be decrypted with the corresponding public key. This feature has several powerful applications, most importantly for SSL, as a way to prove identity. Imagine, as in figure 2-6, that Bob encrypts some well-known information using his private key and sends the resulting ciphertext to Alice. Alice can use Bob's public key to decipher the information. She then compares the result with the well-known information she was expecting. If there is a match, then Alice is assured that the information was encrypted with Bob's private key. Only that key would have yielded the successful decryption. And, since Bob is the only person who knows his private key, Alice is further assured that Bob was the

Figure 2-6 Public key ciphers verify identity using published keys.

one who sent the information. Through this approach, Bob has proven his identity to Alice.

Reversible public key algorithms such as RSA can also provide another important service: the digital equivalent of a signature. Suppose that Bob needs information from Alice. And further suppose that it is important that Alice not be able to later deny sending him the information, either to Bob or to an independent third party (such as a judge). In effect, Bob needs Alice to *sign* the information. To accomplish this, Alice can encrypt the information with her private key. Since anyone can obtain her public key, anyone can decipher the information. Only Alice, however, knows her private key, so only Alice could have encrypted the information in the first place.

Some public key algorithms can only be used for digital signatures; they cannot provide encryption services. One such algorithm important to SSL is the Digital Signature Algorithm (DSA).

2.2.3   Combining Secret and Public Key Cryptography

Public key encryption is a powerful tool, but in most practical implementations it suffers from one serious disadvantage—the encryption operation is extremely complex. Complex mathematical operations can place a strain on some systems, requiring more processing capacity than the systems would otherwise need. If there were no alternatives, then most implementations requiring security might accept the higher system cost; fortunately, there is a relatively simple way to get the benefits of public key encryption while avoiding most of the system performance costs. The optimum approach uses a combination of secret key and public key cryptography.

Figure 2-7 shows how this combination can work in practice. To begin, Bob creates a public and private key, and then he publicizes the public key. He does not share the private key with anyone. Alice, who wishes to send confidential data to Bob, retrieves his public key. She also generates a collection of random numbers. Once Alice has Bob's public key, she encrypts those random numbers and sends them to Bob. Since only Bob has his private key, only Bob can decipher Alice's message and extract the random numbers.

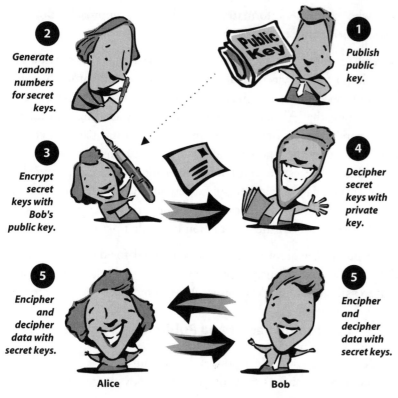

2 — Generate random numbers for secret keys.

1 — Publish public key.

3 — Encrypt secret keys with Bob's public key.

4 — Decipher secret keys with private key.

5 — Encipher and decipher data with secret keys.

5 — Encipher and decipher data with secret keys.

Alice   Bob

Figure 2-7 Effective security combines secret and public key techniques.

Once Alice and Bob have successfully exchanged the random numbers, they no longer need public key encryption. Instead, they can use the random numbers as secret keys for standard symmetric encryption. Alice and Bob can communicate securely as long as they wish. And since symmetric encryption does not need nearly as much processing power as asymmetric encryption, the encryption comes at a much lower cost.

There is an important variation to this process that relies on a different type of public key algorithm. The special type of algorithm is known as a *key exchange algorithm*, and the most famous example is the Diffie-Hellman algorithm. Diffie-Hellman is usually thought of as a public key algorithm, even though it cannot be used for encryption or for digital signatures. Rather, Diffie-Hellman allows two parties to securely establish a secret number using only public messages. Diffie-Hellman is an alternative to steps 1–4 of figure 2-7.

One final note on figure 2-7: As the next chapter details, this is actually a simplified view of basic SSL operation. Figure 3-1 shows a different version of the same process.

2.3 Key Management

Key management is a challenge to all forms of cryptography. Public key cryptography improves the situation; at least the keys that the parties exchange do not have to be kept secret from the rest of the world. Still, the public key must be exchanged reliably.

In the previous examples, Alice has hypothetically retrieved Bob's public keys from the newspaper. Suppose, however, that the nefarious Charles was able to print a phony newspaper (with a phony public key for Bob) and sneak it into Alice's driveway in the morning in place of her real paper. How would Alice know of the fraud?

It is exactly this problem that has led to the creation of public key certificates and certificate authorities. Although unnoticed by most casual Internet users, these are critical to the Secure Sockets Layer protocol and Web commerce.

2.3.1 Public Key Certificates

In many ways, public key certificates are the digital equivalent of a driver's license. Although certificates may belong to computer systems instead of individuals, they share three important characteristics with driver's licenses. First, they each identify their subjects by including the subjects' names. Second, they assert key information about the subject. A driver's license declares that the subject has certain privileges (i.e., driving a car), while a certificate affirms the subject's public key (and perhaps other privileges). Finally, both a certificate and a driver's license are issued by a trusted organization, either a governmental agency or a certificate authority.

Figure 2-8 shows the contents of a typical public key certificate. Appendix A discusses this particular certificate format in detail, but only a few of the fields are truly important. The first of those is the *issuer* field, which identifies the organization that has issued the certificate. This information is critical to a person or computer system that examines a certificate because it determines whether the certificate can be trusted. The next important field is the *period of validity*. Like driver's licenses, certificates expire after a certain time. The next field identifies the *subject* of the certificate, and it is followed by the *subject's public key*.

The final field of the certificate is also important. That field is the issuer's *signature*, which is a digital signature of the contents of the certificate. The issuer creates this signature by encrypting a hash of the certificate with its private key. Any system that knows the issuer's public key can verify the signature and ensure the validity of the certificate. Since this field can be a bit confusing, it is worthwhile to emphasize that the *issuer* creates the signature using its own private key, while the certificate itself contains the *subject's* public key.

Version
Serial Number
Algorithm Identifier
Issuer
Period of Validity
Subject
Subject's Public Key
Issuer Unique ID
Subject Unique ID
Extensions
Signature

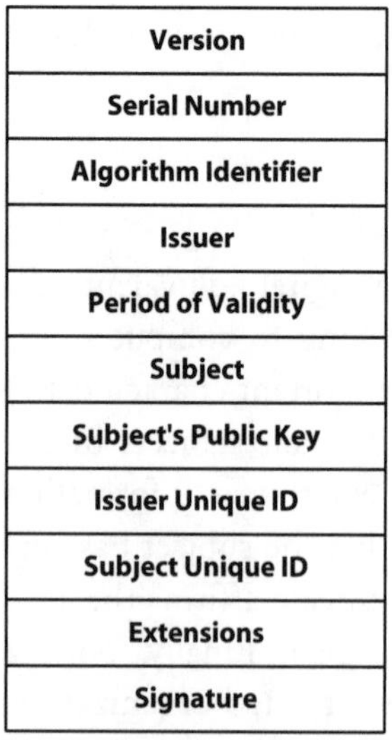

Figure 2-8 A public key certificate validates a subject's public key.

2.3.2   Certificate Authorities

The issuer of a public key certificate is traditionally known as a *certificate authority* (CA), and certificate authorities play a vital role in establishing trust among a community of users. As the previous subsection indicates, the certificate authority digitally signs all certificates, attesting to the validity of the public keys they contain. If users trust the certificate authority, they can trust any certificate that CA issues.

In many cases, a certificate authority can be identified as either a private or a public CA. Private authorities include organizations that issue certificates strictly for their own users. A corporation, for example, may issue public key certificates for its employees. (Actually, they would issue the certificates for the employees' computers.) The company could then set up its internal network to require appropriate certificates before granting access to critical data. Although systems within the company's computer network could trust the company's certificates, outside systems, including, for example, public Web servers, would be unlikely to do so. A private certificate authority issues certificates for use on its own private networks.

But the Internet is a public network, and Web security generally relies on public certificate authorities. A public certificate authority issues certificates to the general public, and it can certify the identity of both individuals and organizations. Public authorities act as the digital equivalent of notary publics, certifying the identity of any party that presents appropriate credentials. For a company that wishes to establish a secure Web site, those credentials may include a Dun & Bradstreet D-U-N-S number, a business license, articles of incorporation, or SEC filings that establish the company's corporate identity.

Certificate authorities are themselves frequently identified by their certificates, but their certificates differ from standard certificates in one important respect: the subject and the issuer are one and the same. The certificate authority certifies its own identity. Figure 2-9 highlights the fact that the public key in a CA certificate is also the public key that verifies the certificate's signature. This is a critical

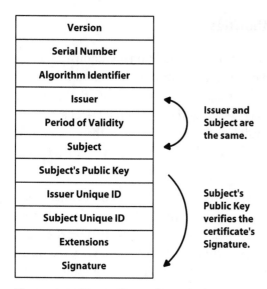

Figure 2-9 CA certificates have the same issuer and subject.

distinction from normal certificates. Any party that receives a normal certificate can check the certificate's signature to decide whether to trust the public key in that certificate. As long as the certificate's signature is valid and the issuer is trustworthy, then the receiving party can safely trust the public key. With a CA certificate, on the other hand, verifying the certificate's signature does not help to establish trust. Any party that could forge a CA certificate would know the forged private key, and could thus easily generate the matching certificate signature. The validity of CA certificates must be established by other methods.

In the case of Web commerce security, the validity of certificate authorities depends largely on the browser manufacturers. Both Microsoft's Internet Explorer and Netscape's Navigator by default recognize the certificates from important public certificate authorities. Figure 2-10 shows some of the certificate authorities Netscape recognizes. (The full list, as of this writing, includes more than 50 authorities.) Although both Netscape and Microsoft allow users to install additional certificate authorities into their browsers, most secure Web sites elect to use a certificate that doesn't require this extra effort from their users.

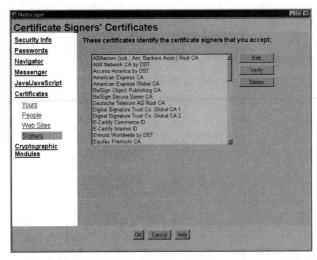

Figure 2-10 Netscape Navigator recognizes many certificate authorities.

2.3.3 Certificate Hierarchies

Sometimes, it becomes difficult for a certificate authority to effectively track all the parties whose identities it certifies. Especially as the number of certificates grows, a single authority may become an unacceptable bottleneck in the certification process. Fortunately, public key certificates support the concept of certificate hierarchies, which alleviate the scalability problems of a single, monolithic authority.

With a hierarchy in place, a certificate authority does not have to certify all identities itself. Instead, it designates one or more subsidiary authorities. These authorities may, in turn, designate their own subsidiaries, the hierarchy continuing until an authority actually certifies end users. Figure 2-11 illustrates a simple three-level hierarchy, one that might occur within a large corporation. As the figure shows, the ACME Corporation has a master certificate authority and two subordinate authorities, one for Human Resources and another for Research and Development. The subordinate authorities are responsible for entities within their domains.

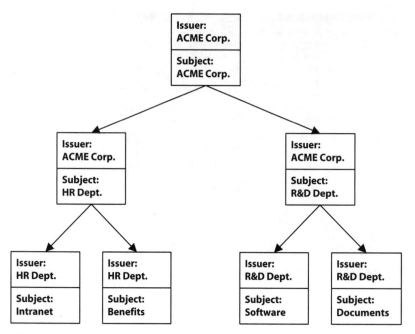

Figure 2-11 Certificate hierarchies divide responsibility for certificates.

A particularly powerful feature of certificate hierarchies is that they do not require that all parties automatically trust all the certificate authorities. Indeed, the only authority whose trust must be established throughout the enterprise is the master certificate authority. Because of its position in the hierarchy, this authority is generally known as the *root authority*.

To see this process in action, consider what happens when a client in the R&D department needs to verify the identity of the Benefits server. The server presents its certificate, issued (and signed) by the HR department's authority. The R&D client does not trust the HR authority, however, so it asks to see that authority's certificate. When the client receives the HR authority's certificate, it can verify that the HR authority was certified by the corporation's root CA. Since the R&D client does trust the root CA, it can trust the Benefits server.

2.3.4   Certificate Revocation Lists

Before leaving the subject of public key certificates, there is one loose end to tie up. So far, we've seen how certificate authorities issue certificates, but what about the reverse process? What happens if a CA issues a certificate by mistake and wants to correct itself? Or what if a subject accidentally reveals its private key, so its certified public key is no longer safe to use? To solve these types of problems, certificate authorities use certificate revocation lists. A certificate revocation list, or CRL for short, is a list of certificates that the authority has previously issued, but no longer considers valid. The certificates themselves still appear legitimate; their signatures are correct, and their validity periods are appropriate. Nonetheless, the CA needs to indicate that they can no longer be trusted. The authority cannot change the certificates since they've already been issued, so the best it can do is maintain a list of these revoked certificates. It is the responsibility of any party that trusts another's certificate to check with the certificate authority to make sure the certificate has not been revoked. This function is not the responsibility of the SSL protocol, so we won't discuss it in any depth. It is noteworthy to consider, though, that the current Web commerce infrastructure does not have an effective (and widely supported) means for systems to check a certificate against a CRL. For that reason, there is no practical way to revoke a traditional Web commerce certificate.

3

SSL Operation

With an understanding of some of the key concepts of cryptography, we can now look closely at the operation of the Secure Sockets Layer (SSL) protocol. Although SSL is not an extremely complicated protocol, it does offer several options and variations. This chapter explains SSL by starting with the simplest case: establishing an encrypted communications channel. It then considers successively more complex options, including authenticating the communicating parties, separating encryption from authentication, and resuming a previously established session. Within these sections, you will discover the full power of SSL.

The SSL protocol consists of a set of messages and rules about when to send (and not to send) each one. In this chapter, we consider what those messages are, the general information they contain, and how systems use the different messages in a communications session. We do not, however, explore the detailed message formats: the bits and bytes that make up SSL messages as they transit across a network. That detail is the subject of chapter 4. Neither do we spend time here on the detailed cryptographic computations SSL requires; those, too, are a topic for the next chapter. This chapter concentrates on the big picture. The details will be much easier to understand once you have an appreciation of the overall operation of the Secure Sockets Layer.

3.1 SSL Roles

The Secure Sockets Layer protocol defines two different roles for the communicating parties. One system is always a *client*, while the other is a *server*. The distinction is very important, because SSL requires the two systems to behave very differently. The client is the system that initiates the secure communications; the server responds to the client's request. In the most common use of SSL, secure Web browsing, the Web browser is the SSL client and the Web site is the SSL server. These same two roles apply to all applications that use SSL, and the examples in this chapter (indeed, throughout the book) will clearly distinguish them.

For SSL itself, the most important distinctions between clients and servers are their actions during the negotiation of security parameters. Since the client initiates a communication, it has the responsibility of proposing a set of SSL options to use for the exchange. The server selects from the client's proposed options, deciding what the two systems will actually use. Although the final decision rests with the server, the server can only choose from among those options that the client originally proposed.

3.2 SSL Messages

When SSL clients and servers communicate, they do so by exchanging SSL messages. Technically, SSL defines different levels of messages, but that topic is best left for Chapter 4. Since this chapter concentrates strictly on functionality, distinguishing between the various SSL levels is not critical. Table 3-1 lists the SSL messages at all levels of the protocol, in alphabetical order. The remaining sections in this chapter show how systems use these messages in their communications.

Table 3-1 SSL Messages

Message	Description
Alert	Informs the other party of a possible security breach or communication failure.
ApplicationData	Actual information that the two parties exchange, which is encrypted, authenticated, and/or verified by SSL.
Certificate	A message that carries the sender's public key certificate.

Message	Description
CertificateRequest	A request by the server that the client provide its public key certificate.
CertificateVerify	A message from the client that verifies that it knows the private key corresponding to its public key certificate.
ChangeCipherSpec	An indication to begin using agreed-upon security services (such as encryption).
ClientHello	A message from the client indicating the security services it desires and is capable of supporting.
ClientKeyExchange	A message from the client carrying cryptographic keys for the communications.
Finished	An indication that all initial negotiations are complete and secure communications have been established.
HelloRequest	A request by the server that the client start (or restart) the SSL negotiation process.
ServerHello	A message from the server indicating the security services that will be used for the communications.
ServerHelloDone	An indication from the server that it has completed all its requests of the client for establishing communications.
ServerKeyExchange	A message from the server carrying cryptographic keys for the communications.

3.3 Establishing Encrypted Communications

The most basic function that an SSL client and server can perform is establishing a channel for encrypted communications. Figure 3-1 shows the SSL message exchange this operation requires, and table 3-2 summarizes the steps in the figure. This section looks at these steps in more detail by considering each message in the exchange.

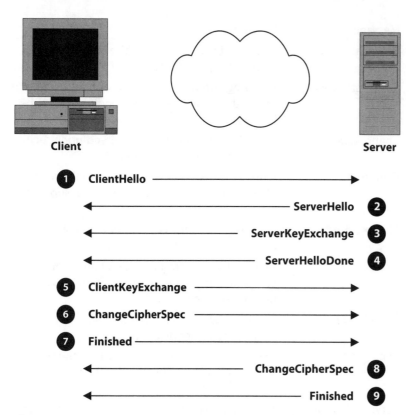

Figure 3-1 SSL uses 9 messages to establish encrypted communications.

Table 3-2 Negotiation of Encrypted Communications

Step	Action
1	Client sends ClientHello message proposing SSL options.
2	Server responds with ServerHello message selecting the SSL options.
3	Server sends its public key information in ServerKeyExchange message.
4	Server concludes its part of the negotiation with ServerHello-Done message.
5	Client sends session key information (encrypted with server's public key) in ClientKeyExchange message.
6	Client sends ChangeCipherSpec message to activate the negotiated options for all future messages it will send.

Step	Action
7	Client sends Finished message to let the server check the newly activated options.
8	Server sends ChangeCipherSpec message to activate the negotiated options for all future messages it will send.
9	Server sends Finished message to let the client check the newly activated options.

3.3.1 ClientHello

The *ClientHello* message starts the SSL communication between the two parties. The client uses this message to ask the server to begin negotiating security services by using SSL. Table 3-3 lists the important components of a ClientHello message.

Table 3-3 ClientHello Components

Field	Use
Version	Identifies the highest version of the SSL protocol that the client can support.
RandomNumber	A 32-byte random number used to seed the cryptographic calculations.
SessionID	Identifies a specific SSL session.
CipherSuites	A list of cryptographic parameters that the client can support.
CompressionMethods	Identifies data compression methods that the client can support.

SSL vs. TLS

The TLS protocol uses a version value of 3.1 instead of 3.0.

The *Version* field of the ClientHello message contains the highest version number of SSL that the client can support. The current SSL version is 3.0, and it is by far the most widely deployed on the Internet. (But see the sidebar for information on TLS.) Note that a server may assume that the client can support all SSL versions up to and including the value of this field. If, for example, a client sends a version 3.0 ClientHello to a server that only supports version 2.0 of SSL, the server may respond with version 2.0 messages that it expects the client to understand. In such cases, that client can decide to continue with the SSL session using version 2.0 functionality, or it can abandon the communication attempt. Section 5.1 includes additional information about compatibility with previous versions.

The *RandomNumber* field, as you might expect, contains a random number. This random value, along with a similar random value that the server creates, provides the seed for critical cryptographic calculations. Chapter 4 has the details. The SSL specification suggests that four of this field's 32 bytes consist of the time and date. The SSL protocol does not require a particular level of accuracy for this value, as it is not intended to provide an accurate time indication. Instead, the specification suggests using the date and time as a way to ensure that the client never uses the same random value twice. This precaution protects against an impostor copying old SSL messages from a legitimate client and reusing them to establish a counterfeit session.

The remaining 28 bytes of this value should be a "cryptographically secure" random number. Security is not something we ordinarily associate with randomness, but it is important in this case. Most computer programs use a technique known as *pseudorandom number generation* to create random numbers. When used correctly, this approach does yield numbers that have the appearance of randomness. However, the technique does have a serious flaw when used in a security context: if an attacker knows the exact algorithm and one random value, that attacker can correctly predict all future random values. This knowledge might allow the attacker to anticipate a particular future value and prepare an attack against it. To prevent this type of attack, SSL implementations should use a different technique for generating random numbers; typically, they use one based on cryptographic algorithms.

The next field in the ClientHello message is *SessionID*. Although all ClientHello messages may include this field, in this example, the field is meaningless and would be empty. Section 3.8 presents an example of how the SessionID field may be used.

The *CipherSuites* field allows a client to list the various cryptographic services that the client can support, including exact algorithms and key sizes. The server actually makes the final decision as to which cryptographic services will be used for the communication, but it is limited to choosing from this list. Chapter 4 describes the format of this field in detail, including the various algorithms and key size options that SSL defines.

The *CompressionMethods* field is, in theory, similar to the Cipher-Suites field. In it, the client may list all of the various data compression methods that it can support. Compression methods are an important part of SSL because encryption has significant consequences on the effectiveness of any data compression techniques. Encryption changes the mathematical properties of information in a way that makes data compression virtually impossible. In fact, if it were possible to compress encrypted data, that would likely indicate a security weakness in the encryption algorithm. For this reason, if two parties are going to employ data compression for a communication, it is important that they compress their data *before* encrypting it. The SSL protocol accommodates this behavior by including the capacity for data compression, and by making sure that the compression occurs before encryption. In the current version of SSL, however, no actual compression methods have been defined. This field, therefore, currently is of limited use. In the future, additional compression methods may be defined and added to the TLS (but not SSL) specifications.

3.3.2 ServerHello

When the server receives the ClientHello message, it responds with a *ServerHello*. As table 3-4 shows, the contents of a ServerHello are much the same as a ClientHello. There are a few important differences, though, which we'll examine in this subsection. In general, where the client makes suggestions in its ClientHello message, the server makes the final decision in its ServerHello.

Table 3-4 ServerHello Components

Field	Use
Version	Identifies the version of the SSL protocol to be used for this communication.
RandomNumber	A 32-byte random number used to seed the cryptographic calculations.

Field	Use
SessionID	Identifies the specific SSL session.
CipherSuite	The cryptographic parameters to be used for this communication.
Compression-Method	The data compression method to be used for this communication.

The *Version* field is the first example of a server making a final decision for the communications. The ClientHello's version simply identifies which SSL versions the client can support. The ServerHello's version, on the other hand, determines the SSL version that the communication will use. A server is not completely free to choose any SSL version, however; it cannot pick a version newer than the latest that the client can support. If the client does not like the server's choice, it may abandon the communication. As of this writing, nearly all SSL clients and servers support version 3.0 of the SSL protocol.

The *RandomNumber* field of the ServerHello is essentially the same as in the ClientHello, though this random value is chosen by the server. Along with the client's value, this number seeds important cryptographic calculations. The server's value does share the same properties as in the ClientHello. Four of the 32 bytes are the date and time (to avoid repeating random values); the remaining bytes should be created by a cryptographically secure random number generator.

The *SessionID* field of a ServerHello may contain a value, unlike the ClientHello's field just discussed. The value in this case uniquely identifies this particular SSL communication, or *session*. The main reason for explicitly identifying a particular SSL session is to refer to it again later. Section 3.8 shows an example of how a client can use this facility to speed up the SSL negotiation process. If the server does not intend the session to ever be reused, it can omit the SessionID field from its ServerHello message.

The *CipherSuite* field (note that the name is singular, not plural, as in the case of a ClientHello) determines the exact cryptographic parameters, specifically algorithms and key sizes, to be used for the session. The server must select a single cipher suite from among those listed by the client in its ClientHello message.

SSL vs. TLS

The TLS protocol uses a version value of 3.1 instead of 3.0.

The *CompressionMethod* field is also singular for a ServerHello. In theory, the server uses this field to identify the data compression to be used for the session. Again, the server must pick from among those listed in the ClientHello. Current SSL versions have not defined any compression methods, however, so this field has no practical utility.

3.3.3 ServerKeyExchange

In this example, the server follows its ServerHello message with a *ServerKeyExchange* message. This message complements the Cipher-Suite field of the ServerHello. While the CipherSuite field indicates the cryptographic algorithms and key sizes, this message contains the public key information itself. The exact format of the key information depends on the particular public key algorithm used. For the RSA algorithm, for example, the server includes the modulus and public exponent of the server's RSA public key.

Note that the ServerKeyExchange message is transmitted without encryption, so that only public key information can be safely included within it. The client will use the server's public key to encrypt a session key, which the parties will use to actually encrypt the application data for the session.

3.3.4 ServerHelloDone

The *ServerHelloDone* message tells the client that the server has finished with its initial negotiation messages. The message itself contains no other information, but it is important to the client, because once the client receives a ServerHelloDone, it can move to the next phase of establishing the secure communications.

3.3.5 ClientKeyExchange

When the server has finished its part of the initial SSL negotiation, the client responds with a *ClientKeyExchange* message. Just as the ServerKeyExchange provides the key information for the server, the ClientKeyExchange tells the server the client's key information. In this case, however, the key information is for the symmetric encryption algorithm both parties will use for the session. Furthermore, the information in the client's message is encrypted using the public key of the server. This encryption protects the key information as it traverses the network, and it allows the client to verify that the server truly possesses the private key corresponding to its public key. Otherwise, the server won't be able to decrypt this message. This operation is an important protection against an attacker that intercepts messages from a legitimate server and pretends to be that server by forwarding the messages to an unsuspecting client. Since a fake server won't know the real server's private key, it won't be able to decrypt the ClientKeyExchange message. Without the information in that message, communication between the two parties cannot succeed.

3.3.6 ChangeCipherSpec

After the client sends key information in a ClientKeyExchange message, the preliminary SSL negotiation is complete. At that point, the parties are ready to begin using the security services they have negotiated. The SSL protocol defines a special message—*ChangeCipherSpec*—to explicitly indicate that the security services should now be invoked.

Since the transition to secured communication is critical, and both parties have to get it exactly right, the SSL specification is very precise in describing the process. First, it identifies the set of information that defines security services. That information includes a specific symmetric encryption algorithm, a specific message integrity algorithm, and specific key material for those algorithms. The SSL specification also recognizes that some of that information (in particular, the key material) will be different for each direction of communication. In other words, one set of keys will secure data the client sends to the server, and a different set of keys will secure data the server sends to the client. (In principle, the actual algorithms could differ as well, but SSL does not define a way to negotiate such an option.) For any given system, whether it is a client or a server, SSL defines a *write state* and a *read state*. The write state defines the security information for data that the system sends, and the read state defines the security information for data that the system receives.

The ChangeCipherSpec message serves as the cue for a system to begin using its security information. Before a client or server sends a ChangeCipherSpec message, it must know the complete security information it is about to activate. As soon as the system sends this message, it activates its write state. Similarly, as soon as a system re-

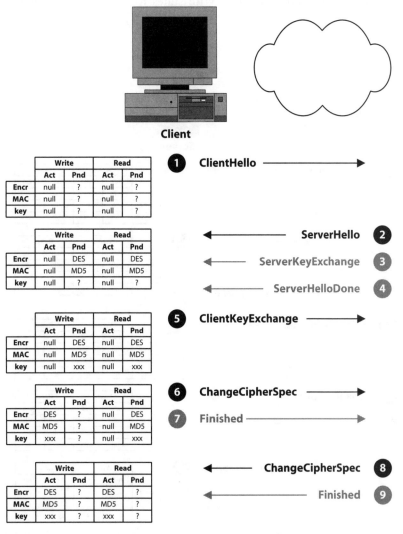

Figure 3-2 Clients build pending cipher suites while using active ones.

ceives a ChangeCipherSpec from its peer, the system activates its read state. Figures 3-2 and 3-3 illustrate this process in more detail. The first shows how the client views the process, while the second takes the server's perspective.

In both figures, the matrices on the side show the systems' read and write states. The events shown in black (as opposed to gray) cause the systems to update their states. As the figures indicate, ssl actually defines two separate read and write states for each system. One of

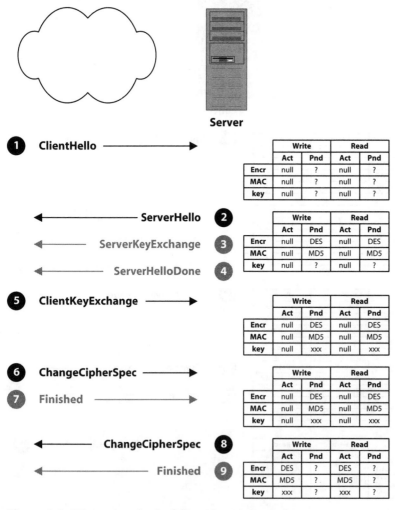

Figure 3-3 SSL servers also build pending cipher suites.

the states is active and the second is pending. Both the client and the server, therefore, maintain a total of four different states: the active write state, the pending write state, the active read state, and the pending read state. (The figures use the abbreviations "Act" and "Pnd" for active and pending, respectively.)

The figures also show the key elements of a state. They are the encryption algorithm (abbreviated "Encr"), the message integrity algorithm (abbreviated "MAC" for Message Authentication Code), and the key material. In figures 3-2 and 3-3, the systems agree to use the Data Encryption Standard (DES) for symmetric encryption and Message Digest 5 (MD5) for message integrity.

As the figures show, all systems start out in active states with no security services whatsoever. This initial condition is necessary for the systems to begin any communication; until they have negotiated security services and parameters, secure communication is not possible. As the systems exchange SSL messages, they begin building the pending state. First they agree on encryption and message integrity algorithms, then they exchange key information. Only then, when both the client and the server have full pending states, can the systems activate those pending states with ChangeCipherSpec messages.

Table 3-5 details the client processing that figure 3-2 illustrates. It describes the steps in the figure that are shown in solid black; those are the steps that result in a change of the client's states.

Table 3-5 Client State Processing

Step	Description
1	When the client initiates an SSL communication by sending a ClientHello message, it sets both of its active states to null (no security); initially, its pending states are unknown.
2	When the client receives a ServerHello message, it knows the algorithms that the server has selected for the session. It updates both of its pending states accordingly. Key information for the pending states is still unknown at this point.
5	Once the client has built and transmitted a ClientKeyExchange message, it knows the key material that will be used for the communication, so it updates the pending states.

6   When the client sends a ChangeCipherSpec message, it moves its pending write state to the active write state and resets the pending state to unknown. No changes are made to the read states. From this point on, all data the client sends will use DES encryption and MD5 authentication as indicated by the now active write state.

8   When the client receives a ChangeCipherSpec, it updates the active read state with the pending values and resets the pending read state to unknown. From this point on, the client will expect received data to be secured with DES encryption and MD5 authentication.

Table 3-6 outlines the processing that takes place in the server. It corresponds to figure 3-3.

Table 3-6   Server State Processing

Step	Description
1	When the server first receives a ClientHello message, it sets both of its active states to null; its pending states are unknown.
2	When the server sends its ServerHello message, it knows the algorithms that will be used for the session, and it updates both of its pending states accordingly. Key information for the pending states is still unknown at this point.
5	Once the server has received a ClientKeyExchange message, it knows the key material that will be used for the communication, so it updates the pending states appropriately.
6	When the server receives a ChangeCipherSpec message, it moves its pending read state to the active read state and resets the pending state to unknown. No changes are made to the write states. From this point on, the server will expect received data to be secured with DES encryption and MD5 authentication.
8	When the server sends its own ChangeCipherSpec, it updates the active write state with the pending values and resets the pending state to unknown. From this point on, all data the server sends will use DES encryption and MD5 authentication as indicated by the now active write state.

Notice from the figures that one system's active write state is the same as the other system's active read state—with one exception. The exception occurs during the transmission of a ChangeCipherSpec message. As soon as one system sends this message, it updates its active states. The other system, however, does not change its active states until it receives the message. In the interim, the two systems are temporarily out of synchronization.

3.3.7 Finished

Immediately after sending their ChangeCipherSpec messages, each system also sends a *Finished* message. The Finished messages allow both systems to verify that the negotiation has been successful and that security has not been compromised. Two aspects of the Finished message contribute to this security. First, as the previous subsection explained, the Finished message itself is subject to the negotiated cipher suite. That means that it is encrypted and authenticated according to that suite. If the receiving party cannot successfully decrypt and verify the message, then clearly something has gone awry with the security negotiation.

The contents of the Finished message also serve to protect the security of the SSL negotiation. Each Finished message contains a cryptographic hash of important information about the just-finished negotiation. Table 3-7 details the information that is secured by the hash. Notice that protected data includes the exact content of all handshake messages used in the exchange (though ChangeCipherSpec messages are not considered "handshake" messages in the strict sense of the word, and thus are not included). This protects against an attacker who manages to insert fictitious messages or remove legitimate messages from the communication. If an attacker were able to do so, the client's and server's hash calculations would not match, and they would detect the compromise. Chapter 4 describes the details of the hash calculation.

Table 3-7 Information Authenticated by Finished Message

- Key information
- Contents of all previous SSL handshake messages exchanged by the systems
- A special value indicating whether the sender is a client or server

3.4 Ending Secure Communications

Although as a practical matter it is rarely used (primarily due to the nature of Web sessions), ssl does have a defined procedure for ending a secure communication between two parties. As figure 3-4 shows, the two systems each send a special *ClosureAlert* to the other. Explicitly closing a session protects against a *truncation attack*, in which an attacker is able to compromise security by prematurely terminating a communication. Imagine, for example, that an attacker was able to delete just the second phrase of the following sentence: "Please destroy all the documents, unless you hear from me tomorrow." The ClosureAlert message helps systems detect such attacks. If a system received the message "Please destroy all documents" but did not receive a ClosureAlert, it would recognize that the complete message may not have arrived. As mentioned, it is not always possible to receive ClosureAlert messages reliably for Web transactions. Appendix b describes other steps Web servers and clients can take to protect against these truncation attacks.

3.5 Authenticating the Server's Identity

Although section 3.3 explained how ssl can establish encrypted communications between two parties, that may not really add that much security to the communication. With encryption alone neither

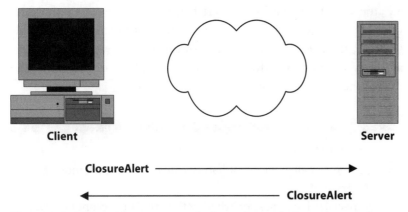

Figure 3-4 ClosureAlert messages indicate the end of a secure session.

party can really be sure of the other's identity. The typical reason for using encryption in the first place is to keep information secret from some third party. But if that third party were able to successfully masquerade as the intended recipient of the information, then encryption would serve no purpose. The data would be encrypted, but the attacker would have all the data necessary to decrypt it.

To avoid this type of attack, ssl includes mechanisms that allow each party to authenticate the identity of the other. With these mechanisms, each party can be sure that the other is genuine, and not a masquerading attacker. In this section, we'll look at how ssl enables a server to authenticate itself.

A natural question is, of course, if authenticating identities is so important, why don't we always authenticate both parties? The answer lies in the nature of Web commerce. When you want to purchase something using your Web browser, it's very important that the Web site you're browsing is authentic. You wouldn't want to send your credit card number to some imposter posing as your favorite merchant. The merchant, on the other hand, has other means for authenticating your identity. Once it receives a credit card number, for example, it can validate that number. Since the server doesn't need ssl to authenticate your identity, the ssl protocol allows for server authentication only. (The protocol does define a process for authenticating clients. Section 3.7. discusses that process.)

Table 3-8 summarizes the actions each system takes to authenticate a server. The same steps are shown graphically in figure 3-5. The process isn't all that different from simple encryption. (Compare figure 3-5 with figure 3-1.) The two messages in black are different when authenticating a server. Those messages, the Certificate message and the ClientKeyExchange message, are discussed next. All other messages are the same as described in section 3.3.

Table 3-8 Authenticating a Server

Step	Action
1	Client sends ClientHello message proposing ssl options.
2	Server responds with ServerHello selecting the ssl options.

Step	Action
3	Server sends its public key certificate in Certificate message.
4	Server concludes its part of the negotiation with ServerHello-Done message.
5	Client sends session key information (encrypted with server's public key) in ClientKeyExchange message.
6	Client sends ChangeCipherSpec message to activate the negotiated options for all future messages it will send.
7	Client sends Finished message to let the server check the newly activated options.
8	Server sends ChangeCipherSpec message to activate the negotiated options for all future messages it will send.
9	Server sends Finished message to let the client check the newly activated options.

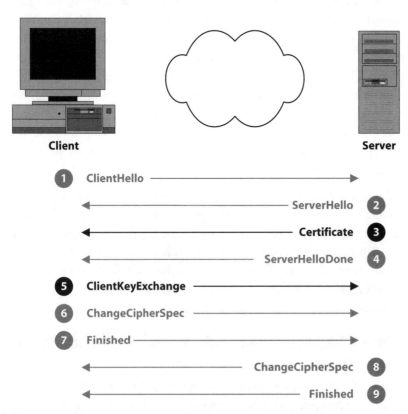

Figure 3-5 Two SSL messages authenticate a server's identity.

3.5.1 Certificate

When authenticating its identity, the server sends a *Certificate* message instead of the ServerKeyExchange message section 3.3.3 described. The Certificate message simply contains a certificate chain that begins with the server's public key certificate and ends with the certificate authority's root certificate.

The client has the responsibility to make sure it can trust the certificate it receives from the server. That responsibility includes verifying the certificate signatures, validity times, and revocation status. It also means ensuring that the certificate authority is one that the client trusts. Typically, clients make this determination by knowing the public key of trusted certificate authorities in advance, through some trusted means. Netscape and Microsoft, for example, preload their browser software with public keys for well-known certificate authorities. Web servers that want to rely on this trust mechanism can only obtain their certificates (at least indirectly) from one of these well-known authorities.

One additional detail in the certificate verification process can sometimes seem subtle, but is nonetheless crucial for real security: The client must ensure not only that the certificate is issued by a trusted authority, but that the certificate also unambiguously identifies the party with whom it wants to communicate. Consider, for example, a malicious company that receives a legitimate certificate from a trusted certificate authority under its own name, but then turns around and uses that certificate illegitimately to masquerade as a competitor. The unsuspecting client that communicates with this malicious company (believing that it is communicating with the competitor) will receive a legitimate certificate as part of the SSL exchange. The client, however, must be intelligent enough to detect that the certificate does not belong to the real competitor. For Web commerce, the key to solving this problem normally relies on the domain name of the server. Respected certificate authorities include the Internet domain name of the Web server in the certificates they issue. And Web browsers check the domain name in certificates they receive against the domain name their users attempt to contact. If,

for example, a browser tries to connect to www.goodcompany.com
and receives a certificate for www.badcompany.com, the browser
knows something is amiss no matter how valid the certificate otherwise appears. Appendix B contains additional information on verifying certificates.

3.5.2   ClientKeyExchange

The client's ClientKeyExchange message also differs in server authentication, though the difference is not major. When encryption
only is to be used, the client encrypts the information in the Client-
KeyExchange using the public key the server provides in its
ServerKeyExchange message. In this case, of course, the server is authenticating itself and, thus, has sent a Certificate message instead of
a ServerKeyExchange. The client, therefore, encrypts its Client-
KeyExchange information using the public key contained in the
server's certificate. This step is important because it allows the client
to make sure that the party with whom it is communicating actually
possesses the server's private key. Only a system with the actual private key will be able to decrypt this message and successfully continue the communication.

3.6   Separating Encryption from Authentication

The previous section explained how a server can send a Certificate
message instead of a ServerKeyExchange message to authenticate itself. One consequence of this approach is that the same public key
information used to verify the server's identity is also used to encrypt
key material in the client's ClientKeyExchange message. This constraint is not always desirable; indeed, in some cases it is actually impossible to support.

The impossible cases are easiest to describe. Some public key algorithms (such as the Digital Signature Algorithm) can only be used
for signing. By their very design, they cannot be used for encryption.
In such cases, it will be impossible for the client to encrypt its ClientKeyExchange information using the server's public key.

This limitation alone would be sufficient to require greater flexibility from the SSL protocol, but it is worthwhile to understand why combining signing and encryption might be undesirable, even when the public key algorithm supports both operations. The most common reason for separating encryption from signing is based not on technical considerations, but on legal ones. Some countries, including important producers of cryptographic products such as the United States (at least at the time of this writing), control the use or the export of products that include cryptography. In particular, the United States makes it more difficult for suppliers to export cryptographic products that use encryption key lengths greater than a certain minimum. (Key lengths less than or equal to these limits are said to

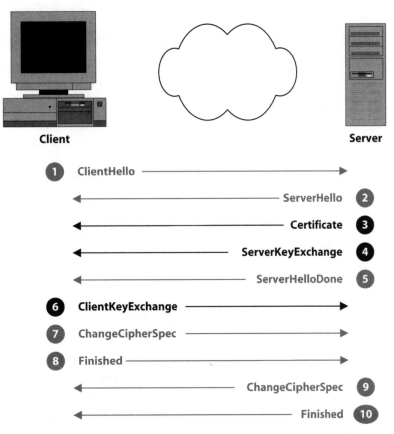

Figure 3-6 Three SSL messages isolate authentication from encryption.

be *exportable*.) In principle, at least, the United States does not impose the same restrictions on keys used for digital signatures. Systems that fall under U.S. jurisdiction, therefore, may prefer to use the longest practical keys for authenticating their identity (thus providing the strongest practical authentication), but use encryption keys that conform to the weaker export restrictions.

Whatever the reason, SSL does provide a mechanism for separating server authentication from the encryption. Table 3-9 outlines the steps involved, and figure 3-6 illustrates the entire process. The figure highlights the three messages that are significant for separating encryption and server authentication. They are the Certificate, ServerKeyExchange, and ClientKeyExchange messages.

Table 3-9 Separating Server Authentication from Encryption

Step	Action
1	Client sends ClientHello message proposing SSL options.
2	Server responds with ServerHello message selecting the SSL options.
3	Server sends its public key certificate in Certificate message.
4	Server sends the public key that the client should use to encrypt the symmetric key information in a ServerKeyExchange; this public key is signed with the public key in the server's certificate.
5	Server concludes its part of the negotiation with ServerHello-Done message.
6	Client sends session key information (encrypted with the public key provided by the server) in a ClientKeyExchange message.
7	Client sends ChangeCipherSpec message to activate the negotiated options for all future messages it will send.
8	Client sends Finished message to let the server check the newly activated options.
9	Server sends ChangeCipherSpec message to activate the negotiated options for all future messages it will send.
10	Server sends Finished message to let the client check the newly activated options.

3.6.1 Certificate

The Certificate message in this example is identical to the example in section 3.5, except that the public key in the server's certificate will only be used to verify its identity. The client still has all the responsibilities section 3.5.1 discussed, however. It must verify the certificate's signatures, validity times, and revocation status, and it must ensure that the certificate authority is trusted, and that the certificate was issued to the party with whom it wishes to communicate.

3.6.2 ServerKeyExchange

The server follows its Certificate message with a ServerKeyExchange message. It is this second message that contains the public key the client should use to encrypt session key information. The ServerKeyExchange is the same message that we saw when no authentication was involved, and the information contained in the message is the same as described in section 3.3.3—with one significant difference: Unlike the example of section 3.3, in which the server keys were sent by themselves, in this scenario, the key information is signed using the public key contained in the server's certificate. This step is essential to give the client a way to verify that the server really does possess the private key corresponding to its public key certificate.

3.6.3 ClientKeyExchange

The client uses a ClientKeyExchange message to finish the negotiation process, just as it does in other scenarios. As before, this message contains the key information for the symmetric encryption algorithm the two parties have selected. Also as before, this information is encrypted using the server's public key. It is important to note that the public key used for this encryption is the public key from the ServerKeyExchange message, not the public key from the server's Certificate message (even if that public key algorithm supports encryption).

3.7 Authenticating the Client's Identity

Since SSL includes mechanisms to authenticate a server's identity, it is natural to expect that the protocol also defines a way to authenticate a client's identity. Indeed, that is the case; the mechanism is very similar to that for server authentication. You can see the whole process in figure 3-7, which highlights the messages that are significantly different from the message flows we've considered so far. Those messages are the CertificateRequest, the client's Certificate message, and the CertificateVerify. Table 3-10 highlights the role of those messages by summarizing the entire message flow. The rest of this section describes them in more detail.

Table 3-10 Client Authentication

Step	Action
1	Client sends ClientHello message proposing SSL options.
2	Server responds with ServerHello selecting the SSL options.
3	Server sends its public key certificate in Certificate message.
4	Server sends a CertificateRequest message to indicate that it wants to authenticate the client.
5	Server concludes its part of the negotiation with ServerHello-Done message.
6	Client sends its public key certificate in a Certificate message.
7	Client sends session key information (encrypted with the server's public key) in a ClientKeyExchange message.
8	Client sends a CertificateVerify message, which signs importation information about the session using the client's private key; the server uses the public key from the client's certificate to verify the client's identity.
9	Client sends a ChangeCipherSpec message to activate the negotiated options for all future messages it will send.
10	Client sends a Finished message to let the server check the newly activated options.
11	Server sends a ChangeCipherSpec message to activate the negotiated options for all future messages it will send.
12	Server sends a Finished message to let the client check the newly activated options.

3.7.1 CertificateRequest

In any SSL exchange, the server determines whether client authentication is required. The client has no choice of its own; it simply complies with the server's wishes. If the server does require client authentication, it indicates that by sending a *CertificateRequest* message as part of its hello negotiation.

As figure 3-7 indicates, the server sends the CertificateRequest after its own Certificate message. Although not shown in the figure, the

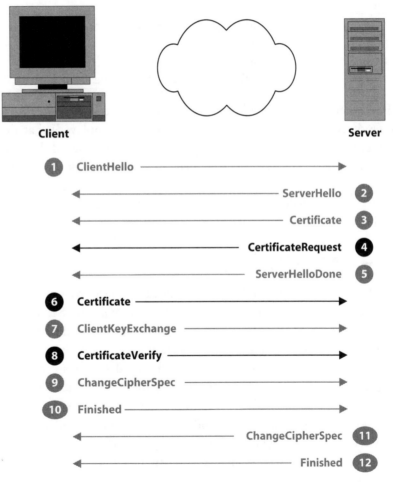

Figure 3-7 Three SSL messages authenticate a client's identity.

CertificateRequest would also follow any ServerKeyExchange message the server sends. Note, however, that the SSL specification forbids a server from sending a CertificateRequest if it is not also authenticating itself (by sending a Certificate message). This restriction ensures that the client will know the server's identity before revealing its own.

The CertificateRequest message contains two fields: a list of certificate types and a list of distinguished names, as table 3-11 indicates.

Table 3-11 CertificateRequest Components

Field	Use
CertificateTypes	A list of certificate types acceptable to the server.
Distinguished-Names	A list of distinguished names of certificate authorities acceptable to the server.

The CertificateTypes field lists the various types of certificates (differentiated by the particular signature algorithm employed) that the server will accept. The certificate types are listed in order of decreasing preference. The DistinguishedNames field identifies the certificate authorities (denoted by their *distinguished name;* see appendix A) that the server will accept. No preference is implied by the order in which the different authorities appear in this list.

3.7.2 Certificate

A client normally responds to the certificate request by sending its own Certificate message immediately after receiving the ServerHelloDone. The format of the client's Certificate message is identical to the server's Certificate message that section 3.5.1 discussed; both contain a certificate chain beginning with the local system's certificate and ending with the certificate authority's root certificate. If a client does not possess a certificate that meets the server's criteria (or if it has no certificate at all), it responds with a NoCertificateAlert. The server can choose to ignore this alert and continue with the communication (though it will be unable to verify the client's identity), or it can terminate the session at that point.

Note that ssl only uses the client's public key for digital signatures. Unlike for the server's public key, there is no protocol function that uses the client's public key for encryption. There is no need, therefore, to explicitly separate client authentication from encryption, so ssl has no client equivalent for the ServerKeyExchange message. (The ClientKeyExchange, as we've seen, transfers symmetric key information, not public key information.)

3.7.3 CertificateVerify

Simply sending a client Certificate message does not complete the process of authenticating the client's identity. The client must also prove that it possesses the private key corresponding to the certificate's public key. For its proof, the client uses a *CertificateVerify* message. This message contains a digitally signed cryptographic hash of information available to both the client and the server. Specifically, the client signs a hash of the information table 3-12 lists. The server also has this information, and it will receive (in the Certificate message) the client's public key. The server can then verify the signature and make sure that the client possesses the appropriate private key.

Table 3-12 Information Authenticated by CertificateVerify Message

- Key information.
- Contents of all previous ssl handshake messages exchanged by the systems.

From looking at figure 3-7, you might wonder why the CertificateVerify message doesn't immediately follow the Certificate message. Instead of this seemingly natural order, ssl has the client send a ClientKeyExchange message between the two. The reason for this message order is based on the cryptographic contents of the messages. The CertificateVerify message relies on cryptographic values that are computed and transferred to the server in the ClientKeyExchange. Until the server receives the ClientKeyExchange, it cannot validate the CertificateVerify message. (Chapter 4 contains a more detailed discussion of the specific computations each side employs.)

3.8 Resuming a Previous Session

As this chapter has demonstrated, establishing an SSL session may be complex, requiring sophisticated cryptographic calculations and a significant number of protocol messages. To minimize the overhead of these calculations and messages, SSL defines a mechanism by which two parties can reuse previously negotiated SSL parameters. With this method, the parties do not need to repeat the crypto-graphic negotiations or authentication calculations; they simply continue from where they left off before. As table 3-13 and figure 3-8 show, resuming earlier sessions notably streamlines the negotiation.

Table 3-13 Resuming a Session

Step	Action
1	Client sends ClientHello message specifying a previously established SessionID.
2	Server responds with ServerHello message agreeing to this SessionID.

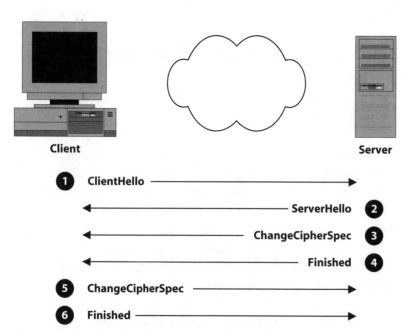

Figure 3-8 It only takes six messages to resume an SSL session.

Step	Action
3	Server sends ChangeCipherSpec message to reactivate the session's security options for messages it will send.
4	Server sends Finished message to let the client check the newly reactivated options.
5	Client sends ChangeCipherSpec message to reactivate the negotiated options for all future messages it will send.
6	Client sends Finished message to let the server check the newly reactivated options.

As the figure indicates, after the server sends it ServerHello message, it immediately sends ChangeCipherSpec and Finished messages. Similarly, the client only sends ChangeCipherSpec and Finished messages once it receives the ServerHello. In both cases, the ChangeCipherSpec directs each party to make the previously active cipher suite active once again.

The key to session resumption is the ClientHello message. The client proposes to resume a previous session by including that session's SessionID value in its ClientHello. (Recall from the discussion in section 3.3.1 that this value is left empty when an SSL session is first established; the server can supply a value in its ServerHello response.) If the server wishes to accept the client's proposal and resume the earlier session, it indicates its acceptance by including the same SessionID value in its own ServerHello. If the server elects not to resume the earlier session, it sends a different SessionID value and the full negotiation then takes place.

Although session resumption offers a great deal of convenience and efficiency to the systems that use it, those systems should exercise some care in employing it. When a single key is employed, encryption inevitably becomes less secure, both as more information is protected and as time passes. Potential attackers gain more data to analyze and more time to perform the analysis. Systems that consider using SSL session resumption should weigh those considerations against the expected efficiency and convenience gains.

4

Message Formats

With chapter 3's description of the various SSL messages and how they're used in mind, it is time to turn our attention to the detailed formats of those messages. Unfortunately, at least for those used to reading protocol specifications, the SSL standard uses a novel approach for describing that formatting, and although concise and easy to present in textual documents, the SSL descriptions may be a bit confusing for many networking professionals. For that reason, we'll use a more conventional approach—pictures—in this chapter.

The SSL protocol itself consists of several different components organized as figure 4-1 illustrates. Four different sources create SSL messages: the ChangeCipherSpec protocol, the Alert protocol, the Handshake protocol, and applications like HTTP. The Record Layer protocol accepts all of these messages, then formats and frames them appropriately, and passes them to a transport layer protocol such as TCP for transmission.

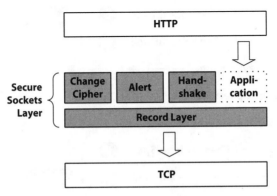

Figure 4-1 SSL consists of several component protocols.

This chapter begins with a discussion of the requirements SSL imposes on the transport protocol. It then describes the details of each SSL component. The final subsections document the cryptographic calculations and options available with SSL.

4.1 Transport Requirements

The Secure Sockets Layer does not exist as a protocol in isolation. Rather, it depends on additional lower-level protocols to transport its messages between peers. The SSL protocol requires that the lower layer be reliable; that is, it must guarantee the successful transmission of SSL messages without errors and in the appropriate order. In all practical implementations, SSL relies on the Transmission Control Protocol (TCP) to meet those requirements.

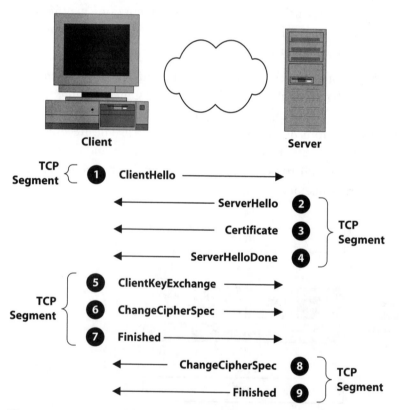

Figure 4-2 SSL can combine messages within TCP segments.

Like all protocols that use TCP, SSL is self-delimiting. That means that SSL can determine the beginning and end of its own messages without assistance from the transport layer. To mark these beginnings and endings, SSL puts its own explicit length indicator in every message. This explicit delimiter lets SSL combine multiple SSL messages into single TCP segments. Figure 4-2 shows a typical SSL handshake sequence. Note that nine separate SSL messages result in only four TCP segments. This combination conserves network resources and increases the efficiency of the SSL protocol.

4.2 Record Layer

The Secure Sockets Layer uses its *Record Layer* protocol to encapsulate all messages. Figure 4-3 emphasizes the Record Layer's position in the SSL architecture. It provides a common format to frame Alert, ChangeCipherSpec, Handshake, and application protocol messages.

The Record Layer formatting consists of 5 bytes that precede other protocol messages and, if message integrity is active, a message authentication code at the end of the message. The Record Layer is also responsible for encryption if that service is active.

Figure 4-4 shows the structure of Record Layer formatting. Table 4-1 describes the figure's individual fields, with the exception of encryption and message authentication codes. Those fields are the subject of section 4.7. In the previous figure, multibyte fields are shown in net-

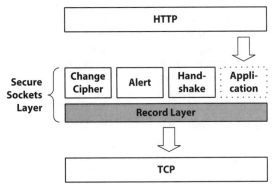

Figure 4-3 The Record Layer formats and frames all SSL messages.

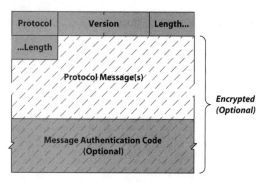

Figure 4-4 SSL's Record Layer encapsulates all protocol messages.

work byte order, sometimes known as *big endian*. Higher-order bytes (those that are most significant) appear first in the figures.

Table 4-1 SSL Record Layer Fields

Field	Size	Usage
Protocol	1 byte	Indicates which higher-layer protocol is contained in this SSL Record Layer message.
Version	2 bytes	The major and minor version of the SSL specification to which this message conforms. The current SSL version is 3.0 (but see the sidebar).
Length	2 bytes	The length of the following higher-layer protocol messages as a 16-bit binary number. The SSL specification requires that this value not exceed 2^{14} (16 384).
Protocol Messages	n bytes	Up to 2^{14} (16 384) bytes of higher-layer protocol messages, including message authentication codes; the SSL Record Layer may concatenate multiple higher-layer messages into a single Record Layer message. Those messages must all belong to the same higher-layer protocol. Also, as a consequence of this potential concatenation, each higher-layer protocol itself must be self-delimiting.

SSL vs. TLS

The TLS protocol uses a version value of 3.1 instead of 3.0.

The SSL specification defines the four different higher-layer protocols that the Record Layer can encapsulate. For any particular message, the Protocol field indicates the specific higher-layer protocol. Table 4-2 lists the values for that field.

Table 4-2 Record Layer Protocol Types

Type Value	Protocol
20	ChangeCipherSpec protocol
21	Alert protocol
22	Handshake protocol
23	Application protocol data

4.3 ChangeCipherSpec Protocol

The ChangeCipherSpec protocol is the simplest possible protocol—it has only one message. That message is the ChangeCipherSpec message introduced in chapter 3. Despite this simplicity, though, ssl treats ChangeCipherSpec as a separate protocol. As figure 4-5 shows, it has the same position in the ssl architecture as other protocols, including the Alert, Handshake, and application data.

At first glance, this approach might seem like overkill. Why not just consider the ChangeCipherSpec message to be part of the Handshake protocol, for example? More careful analysis, however, reveals that ChangeCipherSpec messages must be a separate protocol. Otherwise, ssl couldn't function. The requirement arises because of the record layer encapsulation. The ssl protocol applies security services such as encryption to entire Record Layer messages at once. The ChangeCipherSpec message, however, indicates a change in those services. (Typically, it activates them.) Since encryption cannot be

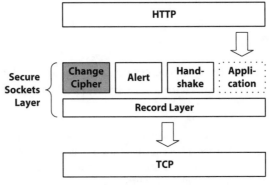

Figure 4-5 ChangeCipherSpec messages are a separate protocol.

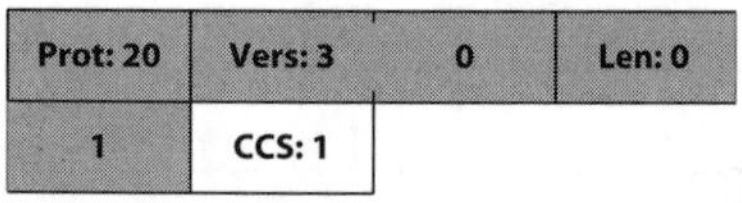

Prot: 20	Vers: 3	0	Len: 0
1	CCS: 1		

Figure 4-6 The ChangeCipherSpec message is very simple.

applied to parts of a message, it is impossible for any other message to follow a ChangeCipherSpec message within a Record Layer message. The most effective way to outlaw such combinations is to define ChangeCipherSpec as a separate protocol, and that is exactly what the SSL specification does.[1]

The ChangeCipherSpec message itself is quite simple, as figure 4-6 shows. The figure also shows how the entire message is encapsulated in a Record Layer message. (The Record Layer header is shaded in the figure.) The Record Layer has a protocol type value of 20, a protocol version of 3.0, and a length of 1. The ChangeCipherSpec message itself consists only of a single byte. It has the value 1.

4.4 Alert Protocol

Systems use the Alert protocol to signal an error or caution condition to the other party in their communication. This function is important enough to warrant its own protocol, and SSL assigns it protocol type 21. As figure 4-7 illustrates, the Alert protocol, like all SSL protocols, uses the Record Layer to format its messages. Figure 4-8 shows the resulting message format. The Alert protocol itself defines two fields: a severity level and an alert description.

4.4.1 Severity Level

The first field indicates the severity of the condition that caused the alert. Alerts can either be warnings (with a severity level of 1) or fatal

---

[1] The SSL specification theoretically allows multiple ChangeCipherSpec messages in a single Record Layer message. That would create the same problems described above. Fortunately, however, there is no practical reason to combine messages that way, so the problem does not arise in real implementations.

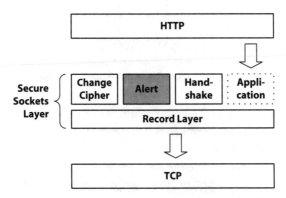

Figure 4-7 The Alert protocol signals error conditions.

(severity level 2). Fatal alerts represent significant problems with the communication, and require that both parties terminate the session immediately. Warning alerts are not quite as drastic. A system receiving such an alert may decide to allow the present session to continue; however, both parties must invalidate the SSL session for any future connections, and they must not try to resume the session later.

4.4.2 Alert Description

The second field in an Alert protocol describes the specific error in more detail. The field is a single byte, and it can take on the values listed in table 4-3.

Table 4-3 Alert Protocol Descriptions

Value	Name	Meaning
0	CloseNotify	The sending party indicates explicitly that it is closing the connection; closure alerts have a warning severity level.
10	Unexpected-Message	The sending party indicates that it received an improper message; this alert is always fatal.

Prot: 21	Vers: 3	0	Len: 0
2	Level	Desc.	

Figure 4-8 Alert protocol messages have only two fields.

Value	Name	Meaning
20	BadRecord-MAC	The sending party indicates that its has received a message for which the message authentication code failed; this alert is always fatal.
30	Decompres-sionFailure	The sending party indicates that it received data that it could not decompress; this alert is always fatal.
40	Hand-ShakeFailure	The sending party indicates that it was not able to negotiate an acceptable set of security services for the session; this alert is always fatal.
41	NoCertificate	The sending party (which is always a client) indicates that it has no certificate that can satisfy the server's CertificateRequest.
42	BadCertificate	The sending party received a certificate that was corrupt (e.g., its signature could not be verified).
43	Unsupported Certificate	The sending party received a certificate of a type that it could not support.
44	Certificate-Revoked	The sending party received a certificate that has been revoked by the certificate authority.
45	Certificate-Expired	The sending party received a certificate that has expired.
46	Certificate-Unknown	The sending party indicates an unspecified problem with a certificate it received.
47	IllegalParam-eter	The sending party indicates that it received a handshake message with a parameter value that was illegal or inconsistent with other parameters.

SSL vs. TLS

The TLS protocol eliminates alert description 41 (NoCertificate) and adds a dozen other values.

4.5 Handshake Protocol

Most of the SSL specification describes the Handshake protocol, as it is the one primarily responsible for negotiating SSL sessions. As figure 4-9 shows, the Handshake protocol relies on the Record Layer to encapsulate its messages. Figure 4-10 illustrates their general format,

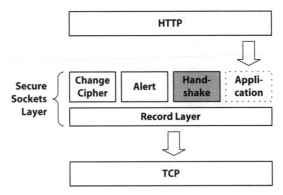

Figure 4-9 The Handshake protocol handles session negotiation.

and indicates that multiple handshake messages may be (and frequently are) combined into a single Record Layer message.

Each handshake message begins with a single byte that defines the specific type of handshake message. Table 4-4 lists the values that SSL defines. The type byte is followed by 3 bytes that define the length of the body of the handshake message. This length is measured in bytes and it does not include the type or length fields of the message. The remainder of this section describes each handshake message in detail. With one exception, the text follows the order of table 4-4. Client-KeyExchange is discussed before the CertificateVerify, since the CertificateVerify message relies on information from the ClientKey-

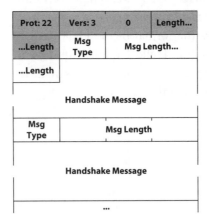

Figure 4-10 Handshake protocol messages may be combined.

Exchange. This approach also follows the order of messages in actual communication sessions more closely.

Table 4-4 Handshake Protocol Types

Value	Handshake Protocol Type
0	HelloRequest
1	ClientHello
2	ServerHello
11	Certificate
12	ServerKeyExchange
13	CertificateRequest
14	ServerHelloDone
15	CertificateVerify
16	ClientKeyExchange
20	Finished

4.5.1 HelloRequest

The *HelloRequest* allows a server to ask a client to restart the ssl handshake negotiation. The message is not often used (and thus does not appear in any of the example scenarios of chapter 3), but it does give servers additional options. If a particular connection has been in use for so long that its security is unacceptably weakened, for example, the server can send a HelloRequest to force to client to negotiate new session keys. Figure 4-11 shows the format of the HelloRequest message. As is clear from the figure, the HelloRequest is quite simple. It has a handshake message type of 0, and, since its message body is empty, its handshake message length is also 0.

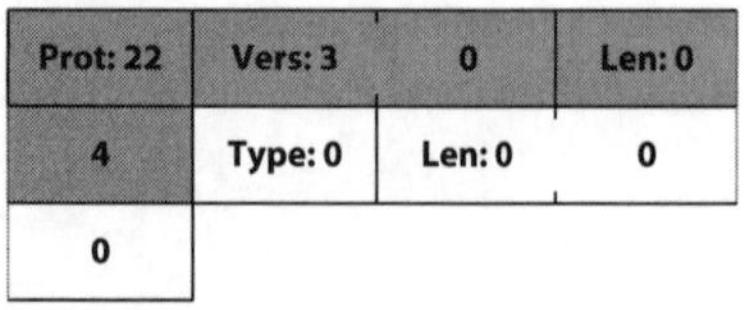

Prot: 22	Vers: 3	0	Len: 0
4	Type: 0	Len: 0	0
0			

Figure 4-11 HelloRequest messages use a simple format.

4.5.2   ClientHello

The *ClientHello* message normally begins an SSL handshake negotia-tion. Figure 4-12 shows the fields that make up a ClientHello mes-sage. ClientHello messages have a handshake message type of 1, and a variable message body size. Two bytes immediately following the message length identify the SSL protocol version. Values of 3 and 0 for this field indicate SSL version 3.0. Although this information is essentially the same as that in the Record Layer encapsulation, in theory, at least, it allows the Record Layer and Handshake protocols to evolve independently.

SSL vs. TLS

The TLS protocol uses a version value of 3.1 in-stead of 3.0.

After the protocol version, the client inserts a 32-byte random num-ber. The SSL specification suggests that clients use the current date and time (up to the second) as the first 4 bytes of this random num-ber, but it does not demand any particular degree of accuracy. Includ-ing the date and time reduces the possibility of duplicating the random value, which, if it were to inadvertently occur, could com-

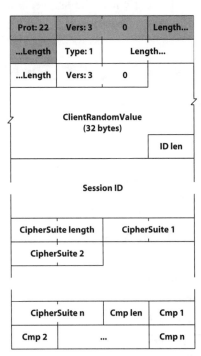

Figure 4-12 The ClientHello message proposes CipherSuites.

promise security. A client, for example, might not be able to remember previous values in between reboots or resets. Including the date and time eliminates the possibility of duplicating an old value (assuming that the reboot or reset process takes at least one second).

The byte after the random value contains the length, in bytes, of the session ID; the session ID itself follows next. Unless a client wishes to resume a previous session, it leaves out the session ID (and sets the ID length to 0). The SSL protocol limits session IDs to 32 bytes or fewer, but it places no constraints on their content. Note, though, that since session IDs are transmitted in ClientHellos before any encryption is enabled, implementations should not place any information in the session ID that might, if revealed, compromise security.

The client's list of proposed cipher suites follows the session ID. The list begins with a single byte indicating the size of the list. The size is measured in bytes, even though cipher suites themselves are 2-byte quantities. A client proposing five cipher suites, for example, would set the CipherSuite length field to 10. Table 4-5 lists the SSL version 3.0 cipher suites; for details on each suite, refer to section 4.7.

Table 4-5 SSL Version 3.0 CipherSuite Values

Value	Cipher Suite
0,0	SSL_NULL_WITH_NULL_NULL
0,1	SSL_RSA_WITH_NULL_MD5
0,2	SSL_RSA_WITH_NULL_SHA
0,3	SSL_RSA_EXPORT_WITH_RC4_40_MD5
0,4	SSL_RSA_WITH_RC4_128_MD5
0,5	SSL_RSA_WITH_RC4_128_SHA
0,6	SSL_RSA_EXPORT_WITH_RC2_CBC_40_MD5
0,7	SSL_RSA_WITH_IDEA_CBC_SHA
0,8	SSL_RSA_EXPORT_WITH_DES40_CBC_SHA
0,9	SSL_RSA_WITH_DES_CBC_SHA
0,10	SSL_RSA_WITH_3DES_EDE_CBC_SHA
0,11	SSL_DH_DSS_EXPORT_WITH_DES40_CBC_SHA
0,12	SSL_DH_DSS_WITH_DES_CBC_SHA

SSL vs. TLS

The TLS protocol, by default, does not include support for the Fortezza/DMS cipher suites, the last 3 listed in the table. In addition, the TLS standardization process makes it much easier to define new cipher suites. As of this writing, dozens have been proposed. In a similar manner, TLS makes it easier to define compression methods.

Value	Cipher Suite
0,13	SSL_DH_DSS_WITH_3DES_EDE_CBC_SHA
0,14	SSL_DH_RSA_EXPORT_WITH_DES40_CBC_SHA
0,15	SSL_DH_RSA_WITH_DES_CBC_SHA
0,16	SSL_DH_RSA_WITH_3DES_EDE_CBC_SHA
0,17	SSL_DHE_DSS_EXPORT_WITH_DES40_CBC_SHA
0,18	SSL_DHE_DSS_WITH_DES_CBC_SHA
0,19	SSL_DHE_DSS_WITH_3DES_EDE_CBC_SHA
0,20	SSL_DHE_RSA_EXPORT_WITH_DES40_CBC_SHA
0,21	SSL_DHE_RSA_WITH_DES_CBC_SHA
0,22	SSL_DHE_RSA_WITH_3DES_EDE_CBC_SHA
0,23	SSL_DH_anon_EXPORT_WITH_RC4_40_MD5
0,24	SSL_DH_anon_WITH_RC4_128_MD5
0,25	SSL_DH_anon_EXPORT_WITH_DES40_CBC_SHA
0,26	SSL_DH_anon_WITH_DES_CBC_SHA
0,27	SSL_DH_anon_WITH_3DES_EDE_CBC_SHA
0,28	SSL_FORTEZZA_DMS_WITH_NULL_SHA
0,29	SSL_FORTEZZA_DMS_WITH_FORTEZZA_CBC_SHA
0,30	SSL_FORTEZZA_DMS_WITH_RC4_128_SHA

The final fields of a ClientHello message list the compression methods that the client proposes for the session. The list begins with a length byte; individual compression methods follow as single-byte values. As a practical matter, though, no compression methods other than the null compression have been defined for SSL version 3. Consequently, all current implementations set the compression length to 1 and the next byte to 0, indicating no compression.

4.5.3 ServerHello

The *ServerHello* message closely resembles the ClientHello message, as figure 4-13 shows. The only significant differences are the value of the handshake message type (2 instead of 1) and the fact that the server specifies a single cipher suite and compression method rather than a list. The values identified by the server are those that the par-

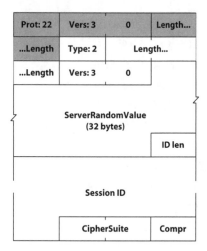

Figure 4-13 The ServerHello message designates the CipherSuite.

ties will use for the session; the server must pick from among the choices the client proposed.

The server may include, at its own discretion, a SessionID in the ServerHello message. If the server includes this field, it will allow the client to attempt to reuse the session at some point in the future. Servers that don't wish to allow a session to be reused may omit the SessionID field by specifying a length of 0.

4.5.4 Certificate

The *Certificate* message is relatively straightforward, as figure 4-14 makes clear. Its Handshake protocol message type is 11, and it begins with that message type and the standard handshake message length. The body of the message contains a chain of public key certificates. That chain begins with 3 bytes that indicate its length. (The value for the chain length is always three less than the value of the message length.) Each certificate in the chain also begins with a 3-byte field that holds the size of the certificate. The message first indicates the overall length of the certificate chain. Then it indicates the length of each certificate with 3 bytes immediately preceding the certificate.

Certificate chains allow ssl to support certificate hierarchies. The first certificate in the chain is always that of the sender. The next cer-

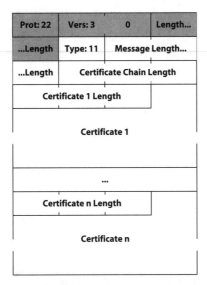

Prot: 22	Vers: 3	0	Length...
...Length	Type: 11	Message Length...	
...Length	Certificate Chain Length		

Figure 4-14 The Certificate message contains a certificate chain.

tificate is that of the authority that issued the sender's certificate. The third certificate (if one is present) belongs to the CA for that authority, and so on. The chain continues until it reaches a certificate for a root certificate authority.

4.5.5 ServerKeyExchange

The *ServerKeyExchange* message carries key information from the server to the client. Its exact format depends on the cryptographic algorithms being used to exchange key information. The various formats—which correspond to Diffie-Hellman, RSA, and Fortezza key exchange protocols—are illustrated in figures 4-15, 4-16, and 4-17. In all cases, the handshake message type has the value 12. Note that there is no explicit indication in the message itself of the particular format it employs. Clients must use knowledge they possess from previous handshake messages (the key exchange algorithm from the selected cipher suite in the ServerHello message and the signing algorithm, if relevant, from the Certificate message) to interpret a ServerKeyExchange message correctly.

The first of the three figures, figure 4-15, shows a ServerKeyExchange message for Diffie-Hellman key exchange. The three Diffie-

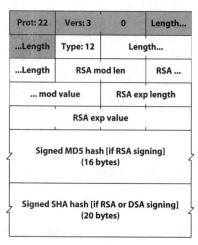

Prot: 22	Vers: 3	0	Length...
...Length	Type: 12	Length...	
...Length	DH p length		DH p ...
...value		DH q length	
DH q value		DH Y$_s$ length	
DH Y$_s$ value			
Signed MD5 hash [if RSA signing] (16 bytes)			
Signed SHA hash [if RSA or DSA signing] (20 bytes)			

Figure 4-15 ServerKeyExchange carries Diffie-Hellman parameters.

Hellman parameters (p, q, and Y$_s$) make up the first six fields after the message length. Each parameter includes its own length, followed by the actual value.

For RSA key exchange messages (figure 4-16), the key information consists of the RSA modulus and public exponent. Each of those parameters is carried in the message as a length, followed by the value.

Prot: 22	Vers: 3	0	Length...
...Length	Type: 12	Length...	
...Length	RSA mod len		RSA ...
... mod value		RSA exp length	
RSA exp value			
Signed MD5 hash [if RSA signing] (16 bytes)			
Signed SHA hash [if RSA or DSA signing] (20 bytes)			

Figure 4-16 ServerKeyExchange carries RSA parameters.

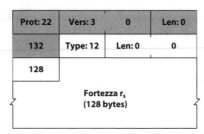

Figure 4-17 ServerKeyExchange carries Fortezza/DMS parameters.

When the systems employ Fortezza/DMS key exchange, the ServerKeyExchange message carries the Fortezza r_s value. Since r_s is always 128 bytes in size, there is no need for a separate length parameter in the ServerKeyExchange message. The handshake message length of 128 is sufficient, as figure 4-17 indicates.

The figures also show that a ServerKeyExchange may include signed parameters. Again, the exact format of those parameters depends on the specific signature algorithm the server supports. If server authentication is not part of a particular SSL session, then no signing is employed, and the ServerKeyExchange message ends with the Diffie-Hellman, RSA, or Fortezza parameters. This option corresponds to the encryption-only scenario of section 3.3.

If the server is not acting anonymously and has sent a Certificate message, however, then the signed parameters format depends on the signature algorithm indicated in the server's certificate. If the server's certificate is for RSA signing, then the signed parameters consist of the concatenation of two hashes: an MD5 hash and a SHA hash. Note that a single signature for the combined hashes is included, not separate signatures for each hash. If the server's certificate is for DSA signing, then the signed parameters consist solely of a SHA hash. In either case, the input to the hash functions (and, thus, the data being signed) is constructed as in figure 4-18.

That data consists of the client's random value (from the Client-Hello), followed by the server's random value (in the ServerHello), followed by the key exchange parameters (either the Diffie-Hellman parameters of figure 4-15 or the RSA parameters of figure 4-16). No signed parameters are included for Fortezza/DMS key exchange.

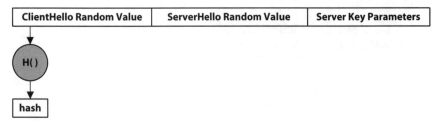

Figure 4-18 The server signs a hash of ServerKeyExchange parameters.

4.5.6   CertificateRequest

To authenticate a client's identity, a server first sends a *CertificateRequest* message. This message not only asks a client to send its certificate (and to sign information using the private key for that certificate), it also tells the client which certificates are acceptable to the server. Figure 4-19 shows the format for this information.

The CertificateRequest message is handshake message type 13; after the handshake type and length, the message contains a list of acceptable certificate types. This type list begins with its own length (a one-byte value), and consists of one or more single-byte values that identify specific certificate types. Table 4-6 lists the defined certificate type values and their meanings.

Prot: 22	Vers: 3	0	Length...
...Length	Type: 13	Length...	
...Length	CT len	CT 1	CT 2
...	CT n	CAs length	
CA 1 length			
DN of CA 1			
...			

Figure 4-19 The CertificateRequest message asks for specific certificates.

Table 4-6 Certificate Types

CT Value	Certificate Type
1	RSA signing and key exchange
2	DSA signing only
3	RSA signing with fixed Diffie-Hellman key exchange
4	DSA signing with fixed Diffie-Hellman key exchange
5	RSA signing with ephemeral Diffie-Hellman key exchange
6	DSA signing with ephemeral Diffie-Hellman exchange
20	Fortezza/DMS signing and key exchange

In addition to certificate types, the CertificateRequest message also indicates which certificate authorities the server considers appropriate. This list begins with its own 2-byte length field and then contains one or more distinguished names. Each distinguished name has its own length field, and unambiguously identifies a certificate authority. For more details on distinguished names, see appendix A.

4.5.7 ServerHelloDone

The *ServerHelloDone* message concludes the server's part of a handshake negotiation. This message does not carry any additional information; it takes the simple form of figure 4-20. The handshake message type is 14, and the message body length is 0.

4.5.8 ClientKeyExchange

With a *ClientKeyExchange* message, the client provides the server with the key materials necessary for securing the communication; the exact format of the message depends on the specific key exchange algorithm the parties are using. The three possibilities that SSL allows are RSA, Diffie-Hellman, and Fortezza/DMS key exchange. Figures

Prot: 22	Vers: 3	0	Len: 0
4	Type: 14	Len: 0	0
0			

Figure 4-20 A ServerHelloDone message ends the server's negotiation.

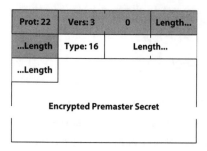

Figure 4-21 For RSA, the ClientKeyExchange carries a premaster secret.

4-21, 4-22, and 4-23 show the message formats for each. Note that the ClientKeyExchange message does not include an explicit indication of the format or key exchange algorithm. Rather, both parties infer the format by knowing the key exchange algorithm of the negotiated cipher suite.

The first message format is for RSA key exchange. As figure 4-21 indicates, the message has a handshake message type of 16, and the standard handshake message length. The message body itself consists solely of the encrypted premaster secret. This premaster secret is encrypted using the public key of the server, as received in the ServerKeyExchange or Certificate message.

The premaster secret is a preliminary step in deriving the master secret for the session. (The master secret, discussed in detail in the next subsection, is the source of all the essential cryptographic data for the session.) For RSA key exchange, the premaster secret is simply 2 bytes for the version of SSL the client supports (3 and 0, for version 3.0) followed by 46 securely generated random bytes.

Prot: 22	Vers: 3	0	Length...	
...Length	Type: 16	Length...		
...Length	DH Y_c length			
DH Y_c value				

Figure 4-22 For ephemeral Diffie-Hellman, ClientKeyExchange carries Y_c.

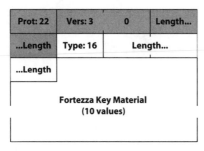

Prot: 22	Vers: 3	0	Length...
...Length	Type: 16	Length...	
...Length			

**Fortezza Key Material
(10 values)**

Figure 4-23 For Fortezza, the ClientKeyExchange carries key material.

When the key exchange protocol is Diffie-Hellman, there are two possibilities for the ClientKeyExchange message. If the Diffie-Hellman exchange is ephemeral, then the message takes the format of figure 4-22. As the figure shows, the message body contains the client's Y_c value, preceded by the length of that value. If the Diffie-Hellman exchange is explicit, then the Y_c value is carried in the client's certificate. In that case, the ClientKeyExchange will be empty.

For Fortezza/DMS key exchange, the ClientKeyExchange message of figure 4-23 requires a set of parameters. Table 4-7 lists the details.

Table 4-7 Fortezza/DMS ClientKeyExchange Parameters

Parameter	Size
Size of the Y_c value	2 bytes
The Y_c value (between 64 and 128 bytes), or nothing if Y_c is in the client's certificate	0 – 128 bytes
The client's R_c value	128 bytes
The Key Encryption Algorithm's public key, signed with the client's DSS private key	20 bytes
The client's write key, wrapped by the Token Encryption Key (TEK)	12 bytes
The client's read key, wrapped by the Token Encryption Key	12 bytes
The client's initialization vector	24 bytes
The server's initialization vector	24 bytes
The master secret initialization vector used for encrypting the premaster secret	24 bytes
The premaster secret, which is a securely generated random value, encrypted by the TEK	48 bytes

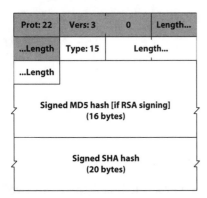

Figure 4-24 The CertificateVerify message contains a signed hash.

4.5.9   CertificateVerify

A client proves that it possesses the private key corresponding to its public key certificate with a *CertificateVerify* message. The message, as figure 4-24 shows, consists of hashed information digitally signed by the client. The exact format of the information depends on whether the client's certificate indicates RSA or DSA signing. For RSA certificates, two separate hashes are combined and signed: an MD5 hash and a SHA hash. One signature covers both hashes; there are not two separate signatures. For DSA certificates, only a SHA hash is created and signed.

In all cases, the information that serves as input to the hash functions (and, thus, is the information that is digitally signed) is the same. Clients build the information in three steps. First they compute a special value known as the *master secret*. Section 4.6.3 describes how this master secret is used in various cryptographic computations; for now, we're only concerned with how systems create a master secret. To calculate the master secret value, the client follows the process given in table 4-8. Figure 4-25 shows the calculation as an equation.

Table 4-8 Master Secret Calculation

Step	Action
1	Begin with the 48-byte premaster secret. The client creates this value and sends it to the server in the ClientKeyExchange message. (See the previous section for details.)

SSL vs. TLS

The TLS protocol uses a slightly different hash calculation for the Certificate-Verify hash; it does not involve the master secret.

Step	Action
2	Calculate the SHA hash of the ASCII character 'A' followed by the premaster secret, the client's random value (from the Client-Hello) and the server's random value (from the ServerHello).
3	Calculate the MD5 hash of the premaster secret, followed by the output of step 2.
4	Calculate the SHA hash of the two ASCII characters 'BB', the premaster secret, the client's random value (from the ClientHello), and the server's random value (from the ServerHello).
5	Calculate the MD5 hash of the premaster secret followed by the output of step 4.
6	Concatenate the results from step 5 to the results from step 3.
7	Calculate the SHA hash of the three ASCII characters 'CCC' followed by the premaster secret, the client's random value (from the ClientHello), and the server's random value (from the ServerHello).
8	Calculate the MD5 hash of the premaster secret, followed by the output of step 7.
9	Concatenate the results from step 8 to the results from step 6.

Once the client has the master secret value, it moves to the next stage in building the CertificateVerify message. The client creates a hash of the full contents of all previous SSL handshake messages exchanged during the session, followed by the master secret, followed by the single-byte value 00110011, repeated 48 times for MD5 and 40 times for SHA. In the third step, the client creates a new hash using the same master secret, followed by the binary value 01011100, repeated 48 times for MD5 and 40 times for SHA, followed by the output of the intermediate hash. Figure 4-26 summarizes the entire process.

master secret = MD5(premaster secret + SHA('A' + premaster secret + ClientHello.random + ServerHello.random))
+
MD5(premaster secret + SHA('BB' + premaster secret + ClientHello.random + ServerHello.random))
+
MD5(premaster secret + SHA('CCC' + premaster secret + ClientHello.random + ServerHello.random))

Figure 4-25 The master secret requires six hash calculations.

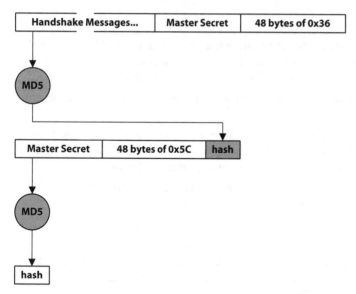

Figure 4-26 CertificateVerify has a signed hash of handshake messages.

4.5.10 Finished

The final handshake message is type 20, the *Finished* message. This message indicates that the SSL negotiation is complete and that the negotiated cipher suite is in effect. Indeed, the Finished message is itself encrypted using the cipher suite parameters. Figure 4-27 shows the format of a Finished message. As the figure indicates, though, the actual contents may be encrypted. When an encrypted message traverses networks, it contents are not visible.

The Finished message body consists of two hash results, one using the MD5 hash algorithm and the other using the SHA hash algorithm. Both hash calculations use the same information as input, and both are calculated in two stages. Figure 4-28 illustrates the process each system uses to calculate the SHA hash for its Finished message. The MD5 calculation is similar.

First, the sender creates a hash of the full contents of all previous SSL handshake messages exchanged during the session, followed by an indication of the sender's role, the master secret, and padding. The sender's role is the hexadecimal value 434C4E54 if the sender is a

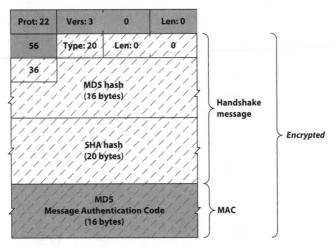

Figure 4-27 The Finished message uses negotiated security services.

SSL vs. TLS

The TLS protocol uses a slightly different hash calculation for the Finished message.

client, 53525652 if a server. The padding is the binary value 00110011o, repeated 48 times for MD5 and 40 times for SHA.

For the second stage, the sender creates a new hash using the master secret, followed by an alternate padding and the output of the intermediate hash. The second-stage padding is the binary value 01011100, repeated 48 times for MD5 and 40 times for SHA.

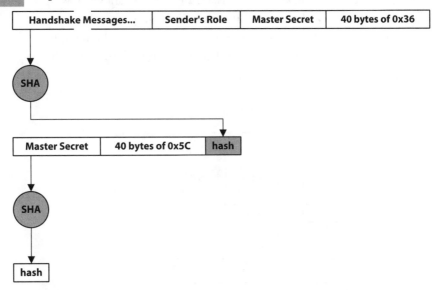

Figure 4-28 The Finished messages includes a signed hash.

Note the similarity between this calculation and the hash calculation for the CertificateVerify message (see section 4.5.9). There are two differences, however. First, the Finished hash includes the sender's role while the CertificateVerify hash does not. (Of course, only clients can send CertificateVerify messages.) Second, the set of handshake messages will be different when the two hashes are calculated. In either case, note that ssl does not consider ChangeCipherSpec messages to be handshake messages (they are not part of the Handshake protocol), so their contents are not included in the hash.

4.6 Securing Messages

The Finished message is the first to actually use the security services that ssl negotiates. Once those services are in place, however, all subsequent messages in the session also make use of them—even additional handshake messages, should the parties want to renegotiate new security parameters. The most important messages, though, are application protocol messages. Those messages contain the actual data that the two parties want to exchange; the security requirements of that data are what make ssl necessary. Figure 4-29 shows how application data fits in the ssl architecture. The ssl protocol provides both encryption and message authentication codes for the data, ensuring that it is kept confidential and that it is not altered. The following two subsections detail each of these services.

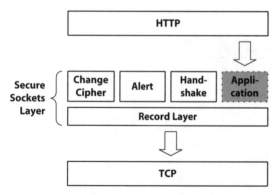

Figure 4-29 Applications use the Record Layer directly.

4.6.1 Message Authentication Code

The Secure Sockets Layer supports two different algorithms for a message authentication code (MAC). As figures 4-30 and 4-31 indicate, those algorithms are RSA's Message Digest 5 (MD5) and the Secure Hash Algorithm (SHA). The particular algorithm for any given communications is determined by the negotiated cipher suite. Other than the algorithm itself, the only difference between the two is the size of the hash. The MD5 algorithm generates a 16-byte hash value, while SHA creates a 20-byte value. In both cases, the hash result is simply appended to the application data. The SSL Record Layer length value includes both the application data and the authentication code. Also, as the figures highlight, both the application data and the check value are encrypted.

To calculate (or verify) the message authentication code, a system uses a two-stage hash very similar to hash computations in the handshake messages. It starts with a special value known as the *MAC write secret*, followed by padding, a 64-bit sequence number, a 16-bit value with the length of the content, and, finally, by the content itself. The padding is the single-byte value 00110011o, repeated 48 times for MD5 and 40 times for SHA. For the second stage, the system uses the MAC write secret, padding, and the output of the intermediate hash. This time, the padding is the binary value 01011100, repeated 48 times for MD5 and 40 times for SHA. This result is the MAC value that appears

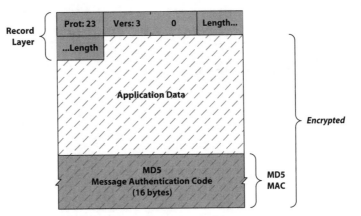

Figure 4-30 The MD5 MAC protects the integrity of application data.

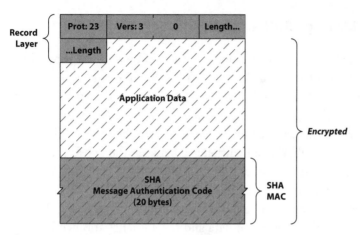

Figure 4-31 The SHA MAC also protects application data integrity.

in the SSL messages. Figure 4-32 shows the process for an MD5 message authentication code.

The two special values included in this calculation are the MAC write secret and the sequence number. Section 4.6.3 discusses the MAC write secret, along with other important cryptographic parameters. The sequence number is a count of the number of messages the par-

SSL vs. TLS

The TLS protocol uses a completely different calculation for the message authentication codes. See section 5.4.3.

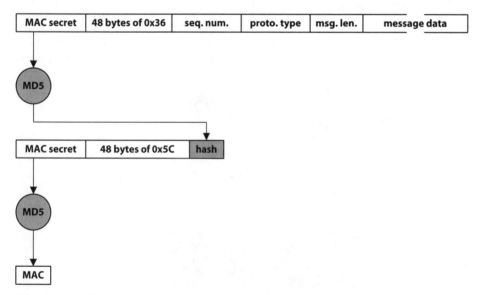

Figure 4-32 SSL calculates a message authentication code in two stages.

ties have exchanged. Its value is set to 0 with each ChangeCipher-Spec message, and it is incremented once for each subsequent SSL Record Layer message in the session.

4.6.2 Encryption

The SSL protocol supports both stream and block encryption ciphers, although the message formats differ slightly. The examples illustrated so far show stream encryption algorithms; they represent the simplest case. Figure 4-33 shows that the information to be encrypted is simply the application data, followed by the message authentication code. With stream encryption algorithms, no other parameters are required.

For block encryption, on the other hand, the data to be encrypted must be a multiple of the block size. And, since application data can rarely be forced into specific sizes, block encryption algorithms rely on *padding*. In this case, padding is used in the sense described in section 2.2.1. Dummy data added to the application data to force its length to be a multiple of the block size. In order to successfully extract the actual application data once the information has been encrypted, the recipient must know where the application data ends and the padding begins. This requirement leads to the format of figure 4-34. As that figure indicates, the very last byte of the encrypted

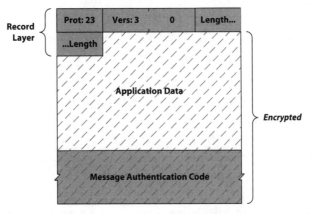

Figure 4-33 SSL can use stream encryption to protect application data.

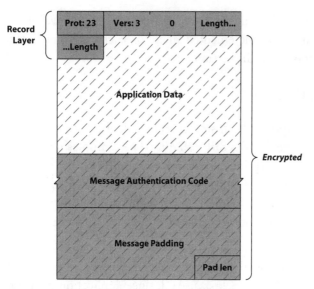

Figure 4-34 SSL can also use block encryption ciphers.

information contains the length of the padding. After decrypting the block, a recipient counts backward from the padding length byte to find the end of application data.

4.6.3 Creating Cryptographic Parameters

The Secure Socket Layer's encryption and message authentication code algorithms rely on a collection of secret information known only to the communicating parties. Indeed, establishing that information securely is one of the three major purposes of the SSL handshake. (The other two are authenticating identity and negotiating cipher suites.)

The starting point for all the shared secret information is the master secret, previously discussed in the context of the CertificateVerify message. The master secret is, in turn, based on the premaster secret. In most cases, the client picks the premaster secret by generating a secure random number. The client then encrypts this value using the server's public key, and sends it to the server in the ClientKeyExchange message. (For Diffie-Hellman key exchange, the result of the conventional Diffie-Hellman calculation serves as the premaster se-

$$\text{master secret} = \text{MD5(premaster secret + SHA('A' + premaster secret +}$$
$$\text{ClientHello.random + ServerHello.random))}$$
$$+$$
$$\text{MD5(premaster secret + SHA('BB' + premaster secret +}$$
$$\text{ClientHello.random + ServerHello.random))}$$
$$+$$
$$\text{MD5(premaster secret + SHA('CCC' + premaster secret +}$$
$$\text{ClientHello.random + ServerHello.random))}$$

Figure 4-36 The master secret requires six hash calculations.

SSL vs. TLS

The TLS protocol defines a completely new process for generating key material. See section 5.4.4.

Once each system has calculated the master secret, it is ready to generate the actual secret information needed for the communication. The first step in that process is determining how much secret information is necessary. The exact amount depends on the particular cipher suite and parameters that the two parties have negotiated, but generally consists of the information that table 4-11 lists. Each party selects from that table the information that is appropriate for the negotiated cipher suite, and then counts the number of bytes each value requires based on the negotiated cipher suite parameters. The result is the size of the required secret information.

Table 4-11 Shared Secret Information

Parameter	Secret Information
client write MAC secret	The secret value included in the message authentication code for messages generated by the client.
server write MAC secret	The secret value included in the message authentication code for messages generated by the server.
client write key	The secret key used to encrypt messages generated by the client.
server write key	The secret key used to encrypt messages generated by the server.
client write IV	The initialization vector for encryption performed by the client.
server write IV	The initialization vector for encryption performed by the server.

To create shared secret information, both parties use a process very similar to the one that yields the master secret in the first place. Figure 4-37 illustrates the approach. They first calculate the SHA hash of

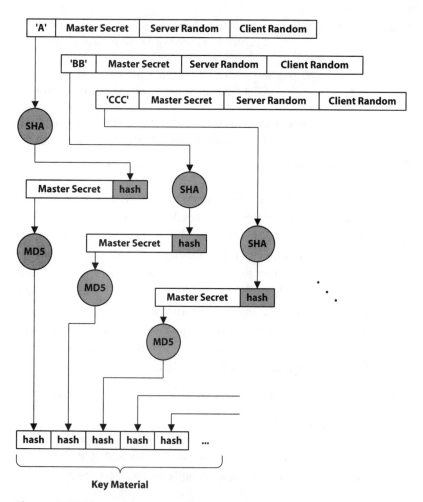

Figure 4-37 The master secret allows SSL to calculate key material.

the ASCII character 'A' followed by the master secret, followed by the server's random value (from the ServerHello), followed by the client's random value (from the ClientHello).

Systems then calculate the MD5 hash of the master secret, followed by the results of the intermediate hash. If the resulting 16-byte value is not sufficient for all the secret information, they repeat the process, but with the ASCII characters 'BB' instead of 'A.' The parties continue repeating this calculation (with 'CCC,' then 'DDDD,' then 'EEEEE,' and so on) as many times as necessary to generate enough secret informa-

$$key\ material\ =\ MD5(master\ secret + SHA('A' + master\ secret +$$
$$ClientHello.random + ServerHello.random))$$
$$+$$
$$MD5(master\ secret + SHA('BB' + master\ secret +$$
$$ClientHello.random + ServerHello.random))$$
$$+$$
$$MD5(master\ secret + SHA('CCC' + master\ secret +$$
$$ClientHello.random + ServerHello.random))$$
$$+$$
$$...$$

Figure 4-38 The master secret seeds calculation of key material.

tion. Figure 4-38 shows the calculations as an equation. The results yield the values of table 4-11 in order, as figure 4-39 indicates.

In many cases, the values of table 4-11 directly supply the secret information needed for the cryptographic computations. One particular class of cipher suites, however, requires an additional refinement. Those cipher suites are known as *exportable*, and generally use smaller key sizes for encryption. (Such cipher suites are said to be exportable because systems that only use such cipher suites are, due to U.S. laws and regulations, generally easier to export from the United States.)

For exportable cipher suites, the final secret key used for messages encrypted by the client is the MD5 hash of the client write key from table 4-11, followed by the client's random value (from the Client-Hello), and followed by the server's random value (from the Server-Hello). Similarly, the final secret key for messages encrypted by the server is the MD5 hash of the server write key from the table, followed by the server's random value, and followed by the client's random value. Note, the initialization vectors are not taken from table 4-11, but are simply the MD5 hash of the client and server's random values

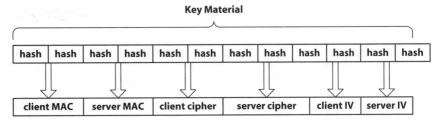

Figure 4-39 SSL extracts secret values from key material.

(for the client write IV) or the server and client's random values (for the server write IV).

4.7 Cipher Suites

Version 3.0 of the SSL specification defines 31 different cipher suites, representing a varied selection of cryptographic algorithms and parameters. Table 4-12 lists those cipher suites, and indicates the key exchange, encryption, and hash algorithms each employs. The first three columns, when combined, form the official SSL name of the cipher suite. The rightmost column marks those cipher suites considered exportable.

Table 4-12 Cipher Suite Algorithms

Key Exchange	Encryption	Hash	Exportable
SSL_NULL_	WITH_NULL_	NULL	•
SSL_RSA_	WITH_NULL_	MD5	•
SSL_RSA_	WITH_NULL_	SHA	•
SSL_RSA_EXPORT_	WITH_RC4_40_	MD5	•
SSL_RSA_	WITH_RC4_128_	MD5	
SSL_RSA_	WITH_RC4_128_	SHA	
SSL_RSA_EXPORT_	WITH_RC2_CBC_40_	MD5	•
SSL_RSA_	WITH_IDEA_CBC_	SHA	
SSL_RSA_EXPORT_	WITH_DES40_CBC_	SHA	•
SSL_RSA_	WITH_DES_CBC_	SHA	
SSL_RSA_	WITH_3DES_EDE_CBC_	SHA	
SSL_DH_DSS_EXPORT_	WITH_DES40_CBC_	SHA	•
SSL_DH_DSS_	WITH_DES_CBC_	SHA	
SSL_DH_DSS_	WITH_3DES_EDE_CBC_	SHA	
SSL_DH_RSA_EXPORT_	WITH_DES40_CBC_	SHA	•
SSL_DH_RSA_	WITH_DES_CBC_	SHA	
SSL_DH_RSA_	WITH_3DES_EDE_CBC_	SHA	
SSL_DHE_DSS_EXPORT_	WITH_DES40_CBC_	SHA	•
SSL_DHE_DSS_	WITH_DES_CBC_	SHA	
SSL_DHE_DSS_	WITH_3DES_EDE_CBC_	SHA	
SSL_DHE_RSA_EXPORT_	WITH_DES40_CBC_	SHA	•
SSL_DHE_RSA_	WITH_DES_CBC_	SHA	
SSL_DHE_RSA_	WITH_3DES_EDE_CBC_	SHA	
SSL_DH_anon_EXPORT_	WITH_RC4_40_	MD5	•
SSL_DH_anon_	WITH_RC4_128_	MD5	

Key Exchange	Encryption	Hash	Exportable
SSL_DH_anon_EXPORT_	WITH_DES40_CBC_	SHA	
SSL_DH_anon_	WITH_DES_CBC_	SHA	
SSL_DH_anon_	WITH_3DES_EDE_CBC_	SHA	
SSL_FORTEZZA_DMS_	WITH_NULL_	SHA	
SSL_FORTEZZA_DMS_	WITH_FORTEZZA_CBC_	SHA	
SSL_FORTEZZA_DMS_	WITH_RC4_128_	SHA	

4.7.1   Key Exchange Algorithms

The SSL specification defines a total of 14 different key exchange algorithms, counting the available variations. Table 4-13 lists those algorithms. For those key exchange algorithms that are part of exportable cipher suites, the table also indicates the size limit that U.S. export policy defines for the algorithm.[2]

Table 4-13 Key Exchange Algorithms

Algorithm	Description	Key Size Limit
DHE_DSS	Ephemeral Diffie-Hellman with DSS signatures	none
DHE_DSS_EXPORT	Ephemeral Diffie-Hellman with DSS signatures	DH: 512 bits
DHE_RSA	Ephemeral Diffie-Hellman with RSA signatures	none
DHE_RSA_EXPORT	Ephemeral Diffie-Hellman with RSA signatures	DH: 512 bits RSA: none
DH_anon	Anonymous Diffie-Hellman	none
DH_anon_EXPORT	Anonymous Diffie-Hellman	DH: 512 bits
DH_DSS	Diffie-Hellman with DSS certificates	none
DH_DSS_EXPORT	Diffie-Hellman with DSS certificates	DH: 512 bits
DH_RSA	Diffie-Hellman with RSA certificates	none
DH_RSA_EXPORT	Diffie-Hellman with RSA certificates	DH: 512 bits RSA: none
FORTEZZA_DMS	Fortezza/DMS	
NULL	No key exchange	
RSA	RSA key exchange	none
RSA_EXPORT	RSA key exchange	RSA: 512 bits

---

[2] During the writing of this book, the U.S. government announced its intention to revise its export policy so as to eliminate these restrictions in many, but not all, cases.

4.7.2   Encryption Algorithms

The SSL protocol supports nine different encryption algorithms, counting variations. They can be found in table 4-14. The table also shows the key material size (derived from the master secret, as section 4.6.3 describes), the effective key size, and the initialization vector size. (In all cases other than FORTEZZA_CBC, the IV size is also the block size.)

Table 4-14 Encryption Algorithms

Algorithm	Type	Key Material	Key Size	IV Size
3DES_EDE_CBC	Block	24 bytes	168 bits	8 bytes
DES_CBC	Block	8 bytes	56 bits	8 bytes
DES40_CBC	Block	5 bytes	40 bits	8 bytes
FORTEZZA_CBC	Block		96 bits	20 bytes
IDEA_CBC	Block	16 bytes	128 bits	8 bytes
NULL	Stream	0 bytes	0 bits	
RC2_CBC_40	Block	5 bytes	40 bits	8 bytes
RC4_128	Stream	16 bytes	128 bits	
RC4_40	Stream	5 bytes	40 bits	

SSL vs. TLS

The TLS standard does not include definitions for the Fortezza/DMS cipher suites. In addition, the TLS standardization process allows for many more cipher suites to be added to the protocol.

4.7.3   Hash Algorithms

The final component of an SSL cipher suite is the hash algorithm used for the message authentication code. Table 4-15 shows the three different hash algorithms SSL defines. It also shows the padding size used in several SSL calculations, including the MAC itself.

Table 4-15 Hash Algorithms

Algorithm	Hash Size	Padding Size
MD5	16 bytes	48 bytes
NULL	0 bytes	0 bytes
SHA	20 bytes	40 bytes

5

Advanced SSL

In the two previous chapters, we've seen how SSL normally operates and examined the detailed format of its messages. This chapter examines some additional facets of the protocol, advanced features that augment its normal operation. Those advanced features include compatibility with earlier versions of the SSL protocol and special support for strong cryptography under U.S. export restrictions. The chapter concludes with a comprehensive explanation of the difference between SSL and TLS.

5.1 Compatibility with Previous Versions

The latest version of the SSL specification is the third major version of the SSL protocol. And, although SSL version 3.0 is well established, some existing systems may support only earlier versions of the protocol. One of the decisions facing developers of current SSL systems is whether to support communication with those older implementations. Adding such support will require additional work, and may result in slightly weaker security. Supporting older versions will provide the greatest degree of interoperability, however. Fortunately, SSL version 3.0 mechanisms can easily accommodate compatibility with earlier versions.

The details of SSL versions prior to 3.0 are outside the scope of this book. However, since compatibility with version 2.0 remains a feature of the latest popular Web browsers, even engineers whose only concern is version 3.0 may find it useful to understand some aspects of version 2.0 compatibility. Network engineers looking at captured protocol traces, for example, may well discover version 2.0 Client-Hello messages crossing their networks. To aid in such understanding, this section looks at how systems negotiate ssl versions, the details of the version 2.0 ClientHello message, and version 2.0 cipher suites.

5.1.1 Negotiating SSL Versions

If a system wants to interoperate with both ssl version 2.0 and ssl version 3.0 systems, one obvious requirement is that the system itself must implement both ssl version 2.0 and version 3.0. It uses the version 2.0 implementation to communicate with other version 2.0 systems, and the version 3.0 implementation to communicate with version 3.0 systems. This simple statement raises the obvious question: How does the system know which is which?

The answer lies in the very first message that the two parties exchange—the ClientHello. The next subsection describes the format of this message in detail, but the essential element of this message is this: a client prepared to support either version 2.0 or version 3.0 sends a version 2.0 ClientHello message. The message is a perfectly legitimate version 2.0 message, but it contains enough hints so that a version 3.0 server, if it's paying attention, can recognize that the client also supports version 3.0. Such a server responds using the ssl version 3.0 protocol, and a normal version 3.0 handshake ensues.

Figure 5-1 shows how this negotiation works when the server only implements ssl version 2.0. Such a server recognizes the version 2.0 ClientHello message, but it is oblivious to the special 3.0 hints. The server treats it like any other version 2.0 message and continues the version 2.0 handshake negotiation. In contrast, Figure 5-2 shows how a version 3.0 server responds. The server is not only capable of understanding the version 2.0 ClientHello, it also understands the special hints. The server, therefore, recognizes that the client is capable of ssl version 3.0. It uses the standard version 3.0 handshake process for the rest of the communication.

The server's responsibilities are fairly simple. If it receives a standard version 2.0 ClientHello (without the version 3.0 hints), it responds

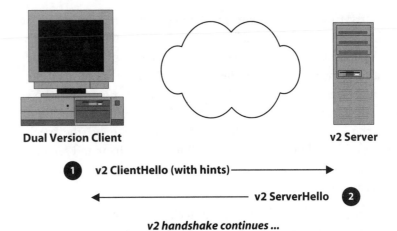

Dual Version Client   **v2 Server**

1 **v2 ClientHello (with hints)** ⟶

⟵ **v2 ServerHello** **2**

v2 handshake continues ...

Figure 5-1 Clients can successfully negotiate with a version 2.0 server.

using SSL version 2.0. If it receives a version 3.0 ClientHello or a version 2.0 ClientHello with the special hints, it responds using version 3.0. Even servers that do not support SSL version 2.0 should still accept and respond to the version 2.0 ClientHello with the special hints. Such servers can reject other version 2.0 messages.

There is one final twist to this process. Since version 3.0 has security improvements over version 2.0, systems should ensure that they're using version 3.0 in every possible circumstance, even when a mali-

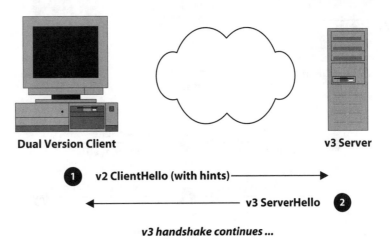

Dual Version Client   **v3 Server**

1 **v2 ClientHello (with hints)** ⟶

⟵ **v3 ServerHello** **2**

v3 handshake continues ...

Figure 5-2 Clients can also negotiate with a version 3.0 server.

cious party tries to trick them into falling back to version 2.0. The most likely threat is from a malicious system that interposes itself between the client and server. During the negotiation phase, it pretends to be a server when talking to the client, then turns around and pretends to be the client when talking to the server. Figure 5-3 shows how such a *man-in-the-middle* attack might unfold. As the figure shows, the attacker modifies the ClientHello to remove the special version 3.0 hints. This modification will force the client and server to use SSL version 2.0, even though both are capable of the newer (and more secure) version 3.0.

The SSL specification defines a special technique that allows two systems to detect the attack if it were to occur. The client takes the first step. When a dual-version client ends up using SSL version 2.0 rather than version 3.0, it uses special padding values in the version 2.0 ClientKeyExchange message. In particular, it sets the last 8 bytes of the padding to the special binary value 00000011. This value indicates that the client could have supported version 3.0. Normal version 2.0 servers will be oblivious to the padding value. Dual version servers

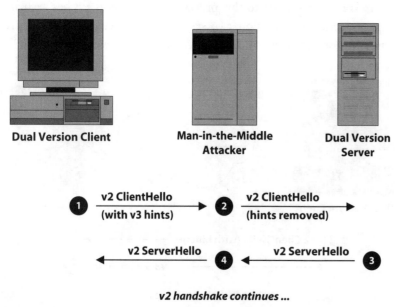

v2 handshake continues ...

Figure 5-3 SSL protects against a version rollback attack like this one.

that receive a version 2.0 ClientKeyExchange, however, can look for the special padding value. If the server finds it, then an attack is occurring. Note that the attacker will not be able to modify the padding (and thus remove the incriminating 00000011 bytes) because the client encrypts that information using the server's public key.

5.1.2   SSL Version 2.0 ClientHello

Even servers that support only SSL version 3.0 may still need to understand version 2.0 ClientHello messages. As the previous subsection indicated, they may receive such a message from a dual version client. The actual message contents are similar to those of the version 3.0 ClientHello, but the format is significantly different.

Figure 5-4 shows a typical version 2.0 ClientHello as a dual version client might build it. As the figure shows, the Record Layer is only 2 bytes, and consists of a protocol type (128 is used for handshake messages) and a single byte for the message length. The actual handshake

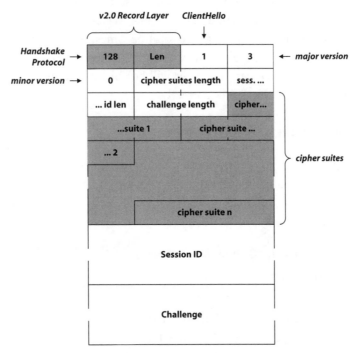

Figure 5-4 Version 2.0 ClientHello messages differ from version 3.0.

message follows, beginning with the message type of 1. This value indicates a ClientHello message. A 2-byte version indication follows. Notice that the version is set to 3.0, even though this is a version 2.0 ClientHello. In effect, the client lies about the version number for the message.

This version number is the hint mentioned previously. It tells the server that, even though the client is sending a version 2.0 message, the client is capable of using version 3.0. A version 2.0 server will be able to parse the message. When it sees a version number greater than it can support, though, it just responds with a version 2.0 ServerHello. That response directs the client to fall back to version 2.0.

The rest of the message is relatively straightforward, but note that version 2.0 cipher suites are 3 bytes in length, rather than 2. This fact provides a convenient way for dual version clients to propose version 3.0 cipher suites within a version 2.0 ClientHello. The client simply prepends a single byte of 0 to the 2-byte cipher suite value from table 4-5. For example, the cipher suite SSL_SSL_RSA_WITH_RC4_128_MD5 (represented in version 3.0 messages as 0,4) becomes, in version 2.0 messages, 0,0,4. Since all legitimate 2.0 cipher suites begin with a value other than 0, a dual version server will be able to recognize the modified version 3.0 cipher suites correctly.

5.1.3   SSL Version 2.0 Cipher Suites

To thoroughly understand version 2.0 ClientHello messages in the context of version 3.0 compatibility, it is necessary to recognize the version 2.0 cipher suites. Table 5-1 lists the values defined in the SSL version 2.0 specification.

Table 5-1 SSL Version 2.0 Cipher Suite Values

Value	Cipher Suite
1,0,128	SSL_RC4_128_WITH_MD5
2,0,128	SSL_RC4_128_EXPORT40_WITH_MD5
3,0,128	SSL_RC2_CBC_128_CBC_WITH_MD5
4,0,128	SSL_RC2_CBC_128_CBC_EXPORT40_WITH_MD5

5,0,128	SSL_IDEA_128_CBC_WITH_MD5
6,0,64	SSL_DES_64_CBC_WITH_MD5
7,0,192	SSL_DES_192_EDE3_CBC_WITH_MD5

5.2 Netscape International Step-Up

One of the challenges facing SSL implementations, and indeed, security products in general, is complying with various laws and regulations that restrict the use of cryptography. The United States, for example, currently treats cryptography like weapons and limits the ability of U.S. companies to export cryptographic products. In principle, the goal of this policy is to avoid letting cryptographic products fall into the hands of terrorists and other criminals, thereby hampering the ability of intelligence agencies to combat such criminals.[1]

The problem is particularly acute for companies such as Netscape and Microsoft. Those companies would like to make their Web browsers as widely available as possible, including making them downloadable from the Internet. Browser developers would also like to include the strongest possible cryptography in their products, however, and those two goals are in direct conflict with each other. Laws and regulations prevent browser developers from exporting software with strong cryptography, including distributing software using the Internet.

Such laws, while perhaps hindering the ability of criminals to commit crimes, certainly interfere with legitimate commerce. A bank, for example, might like to offer banking services over the Internet, even to customers outside the United States. Potential customers might balk, however, if they knew that their Web transactions were secured only by the deliberately weakened cryptography required to satisfy U.S. export laws.

---

[1] During the writing of this book, the U.S. government announced its intention to revise its export policy so as to eliminate these restrictions in many, but not all, cases.

Both Netscape and Microsoft have worked with the u.s. government to develop a compromise approach. The Netscape approach is known as *International Step-Up*, and it is the subject of this section. (Microsoft's very similar *Server Gated Cryptography* is the topic of the next section.)

5.2.1 Server Components

International Step-Up requires no changes at all to an ssl server implementation. The server simply responds normally to all ssl version 3.0 messages. The server does supply a critical element in the International Step-Up process, though—a special International Step-Up certificate. Note that the ssl protocol itself does not address the contents of public key certificates. It simply carries them (whatever their contents) in Certificate messages.

International Step-Up server certificates are special in two important ways. First, they contain a special attribute in the extended key usage (extKeyUsage) field. Appendix a discusses this field (and certificates in general) in more detail, but the special attribute for Netscape's International Step-Up includes the object identifier value of 2.16.840 .1.113730.4.1. The second important characteristic of International Step-Up server certificates is the certificate authority that issues them. All such certificates must be issued under the VeriSign Class 3 authority. (In theory, it would be possible for any authority to issue International Step-Up certificates; however, as of this writing, Netscape's web browser clients are pre-configured to only recognize VeriSign as a legitimate International Step-Up certificate authority.)

5.2.2 Client Components

Most of the action with International Step-Up happens in the client. Clients that wish to use International Step-Up are generally those that have been licensed for export (otherwise, they would not be subject to export laws restricting the strength of their cryptography). Such clients are not free to use strong cryptography in all cases. If they support International Step-Up, however, the client has a latent capability to support strong cryptography. The client is designed to keep this capability hidden from normal servers (thus it conforms to u.s. export regulations), but when it recognizes a server's International Step-Up certificate, it reveals its hidden capability and negotiates strong cryptography.

Figure 5-5 shows the complete message exchange. Note that in message 1, the client only proposes to support export strength encryption. The client does this even though it is actually capable of stronger encryption; clients must do this to obtain the necessary u.s. export licenses. The server has no choice but to select a cipher suite from among those proposed by the client, so the ServerHello message will indicate export-strength encryption. (At this point, the server does not know that the client supports International Step-Up.)

Once the client receives message 3, however, it knows that the server is capable of supporting International Step-Up. It continues with the regular handshake negotiation (messages 4 through 9), but instead of beginning the exchange of application data, it starts a new negotiation with a second ClientHello message (message 10). This message proposes full-strength cipher suites. The server responds to this appropriately, and at the end of the second handshake with message 18, both parties have negotiated a full-strength cipher suite.

5.2.3   Controlling Full-Strength Encryption

International Step-Up is a compromise between the needs of the u.s. government to limit the use of full-strength cryptography abroad and the desire of browser manufactures to offer the strongest possible product to the widest possible audience. Because the u.s. government has verified that Netscape's Web browser only renegotiates full-strength cryptography *after* the server has produced a special International Step-Up certificate, Netscape is free to distribute its browser worldwide, even by Internet download. Controlling the use of full-strength encryption becomes a matter of controlling the issuance of International Step-Up certificates. Currently, only one certificate authority (VeriSign) is able to issue International Step-Up certificates, and the u.s. government controls which companies are allowed to purchase those certificates.

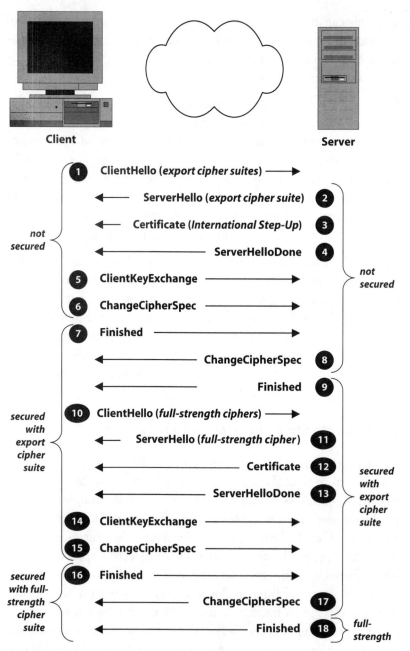

Figure 5-5 International Step-Up negotiates cipher suites twice.

5.3 Microsoft Server Gated Cryptography

Microsoft's Internet Explorer has a capability very similar to Netscape's International Step-Up. Microsoft calls its technology *Server Gated Cryptography* (SGC), which reflects the role the server plays in enabling the client to use full-strength cryptography.

The principles behind Server Gated Cryptography are identical to those of International Step-Up. Clients begin a negotiation by proposing only export-strength cipher suites. When they see a special object in the server's certificate, however, they renegotiate the cipher suite using full-strength encryption algorithms. There are, however, two important details in which Server Gated Cryptography differs from International Step-Up: the specific object identifier in the server certificate and the exact mechanism the client uses to renegotiate the handshake.

5.3.1 Server Gated Cryptography Certificates

Like International Step-Up, servers that qualify for Server Gated Cryptography use certificates with a special object identifier in the extended key usage field. The particular value for SGC is 1.3.6.1.4.1.-311.10.3.3. Equally important, those certificates are issued by a certificate authority approved by U.S. export regulators. As of this writing, the only authority that has the necessary approval is VeriSign, the same authority that issues International Step-Up certificates. In fact, VeriSign does not issue separate certificates for International Step-Up and Server Gated Cryptography. It issues a single certificate, which VeriSign calls a *Global Secure ID*, that has both extended key usage objects included in it. The same server certificate, therefore, supports both International Step-Up and Server Gated Cryptography.

5.3.2 Cipher Suite Renegotiation

Another difference between Server Gated Cryptography and International Step-Up is the approach used to renegotiate the cipher suite

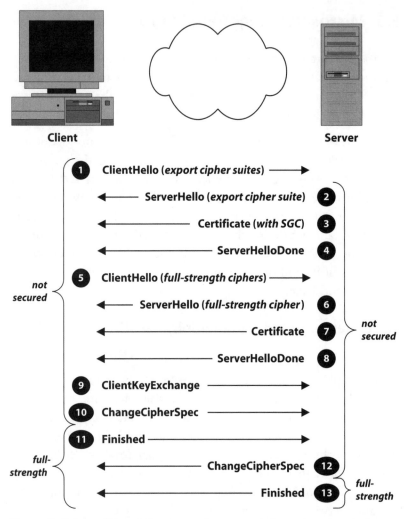

Figure 5-6 Server Gated Cryptography resets cipher suite negotiation.

to a full-strength version. Figure 5-6 shows the sequence of messages for Server Gated Cryptography.

A comparison with figure 5-5 shows that the key difference begins with step 5. While International Step-Up completes the initial handshake for export-strength ciphers and renegotiates after that handshake is complete, Server Gated Cryptography effectively aborts the initial handshake and sends a new ClientHello message at step 5. This new ClientHello proposes stronger encryption parameters, allowing the server to select full-strength security for the session.

Two aspects of this approach to cipher suite renegotiation are worth elaboration. First, some of the documentation on Server Gated Cryptography available from Microsoft appears to imply that a special "reset" message precedes the second ClientHello of step 5. This is not the case, at least with versions 4.01 and 5.0 of Internet Explorer. The client simply sends a new ClientHello as soon as it receives the ServerHelloDone. There is nothing special about this ClientHello message. (It does not, for example, include a TCP reset.) With Server Gated Cryptography, any "reset" is merely implied by the second ClientHello. Second, the SSL standard is not completely clear as to whether the SGC approach is permitted. It is not clearly illegal, however, and it does work appropriately. Given the widespread deployment of Internet Explorer and Microsoft Web servers, the point is probably academic anyway.

5.4 The Transport Layer Security Protocol

Although the Secure Sockets Layer protocol was originally developed primarily by Netscape, the protocol has become so critical to the operation of the Internet that the Internet Engineering Task Force (IETF) has, with Netscape's blessing, taken over future development of SSL standards. For several reasons, including a desire to more clearly distinguish SSL from ongoing work with the IP Security (IPSEC) protocol, the IETF rechristened the protocol with the name *Transport Layer Security*, or TLS.

The TLS specification represents a relatively modest, incremental improvement to the SSL protocol. There is far less difference, for example, between SSL version 3.0 and TLS than there is between SSL versions 2.0 and 3.0. In fact, there are really only a few significant changes between SSL and TLS, which table 5-2 summarizes. The remainder of this section details these changes in seven subsections, which correspond to the items in table 5-2.

Table 5-2 Differences between SSL and TLS

	SSL v3.0	TLS v1.0
Protocol version in messages	3.0	3.1
Alert protocol message types	12	23
Message authentication	ad hoc	standard
Key material generation	ad hoc	PRF
CertificateVerify	complex	simple
Finished	ad hoc	PRF
Baseline cipher suites	includes Fortezza	no Fortezza

5.4.1   TLS Protocol Version

Perhaps it is unfortunate that the IETF decided to rename SSL to TLS. That decision has certainly introduced some confusion in the version numbers for the TLS protocol. The existing Transport Layer Security standard is named version 1.0. Indeed, it is the first version of TLS. However, in order to maintain interoperability with SSL version 3.0 systems (see section 5.4.8), the protocol version reported in the actual protocol messages must be *greater* than 3.0. Because TLS is a modest rather than a drastic improvement over SSL, TLS designers have specified that the protocol version that appears in TLS messages be 3.1. Presumably, should TLS ever undergo a major revision itself, the new protocol would be named version 2.0, but would be indicated in the protocol messages as 4.0.

5.4.2   Alert Protocol Message Types

One of the areas in which TLS improves on SSL is in its procedures for notification of potential and actual security alerts. In particular, TLS defines almost twice as many alert descriptions. Table 5-3 provides the complete list of TLS alerts. It also marks which of those are new to TLS (with a bullet in the leftmost column), and it emphasizes the fact that alert description 41 (NoCertificate) was deleted in TLS. The TLS specification removed this alert because, in practice, it was difficult to implement. Successfully interpreting the NoCertificate alert requires a high level of synchronization between the Alert and

Handshake protocols, a synchronization that is otherwise not needed. To eliminate the requirement for this synchronization, TLS has clients that do not have appropriate certificates simply return an empty Certificate message.

Table 5-3 TLS Alert Descriptions

	Value	Name	Meaning
	0	CloseNotify	The sending party indicates explicitly that it is closing the connection; closure alerts have a warning severity level.
	10	Unexpect-edMessage	The sending party indicates that it received an improper message; this alert is always fatal.
	20	BadRecord-MAC	The sending party indicates that it received a message with a bad message authentication code; this alert is always fatal.
•	21	Decryption-Failed	The sending party indicates that a message it decrypted was invalid (e.g., it was not a multiple of the block size or had invalid padding); this alert is always fatal.
•	22	RecordOver-flow	The sending party indicates that a message it received was, after decryption or decompression, more than $2^{14}+2048$ bytes; this message is always fatal.
	30	Decompres-sionFailure	The sending party indicates that it received data that it could not decompress; this alert is always fatal.
	40	Hand-ShakeFailure	The sending party indicates that it was not able to negotiate an acceptable set of security services for the session; this alert is always fatal.
	~~41~~	~~NoCertificate~~	~~The sending party (which is always a client) indicates that it has no certificate that can satisfy the server's CertificateRequest.~~
	42	BadCertifi-cate	The sending party received a certificate that was corrupt (e.g., its signature could not be verified).
	43	Unsupport-edCertificate	The sending party received a certificate of a type that it could not support.

Value	Name	Meaning
44	Certificate-Revoked	The sending party received a certificate that has been revoked by the certificate authority.
45	Certificate-Expired	The sending party received a certificate that has expired.
46	Certificate-Unknown	The sending party indicates an unspecified problem with a received certificate.
47	IllegalParameter	The sending party indicates that it received a handshake message with a parameter value that was illegal or inconsistent with other parameters.
• 48	UnknownCA	The sending party indicates that it could not identify or does not trust the certificate authority of a received certificate chain; this message is always fatal.
• 49	Access-Denied	The sending party indicates that the party identified in the peer's certificate does not have access rights to continue negotiation; this error is always fatal.
• 50	DecodeError	The sending party indicates that a received message could not be decoded because a field value was out of the permitted range or the message length was invalid; this message is always fatal.
• 51	DecryptError	The sending party indicates that a cryptographic operation essential to the handshake negotiation failed.
• 60	ExportRestriction	The sending party indicates that it detected a negotiation parameter not in compliance with applicable U.S. export restrictions; this message is always fatal.
• 70	Protocol-Version	The sending party indicates that it cannot support the requested TLS protocol version; this message is always fatal.
• 71	Insufficient-Security	The sending party (always a server) indicates that it requires cipher suites more secure than those supported by the client; this message is always fatal.

Value	Name	Meaning
● 80	InternalError	The sending party indicates that an error local to its operation and independent of the TLS protocol (such as a memory allocation failure) makes it impossible to continue; this message is always fatal.
● 90	UserCanceled	The sending party indicates that it wishes to cancel the handshake negotiation for reasons other than a protocol failure; this message is typically a warning and should be followed by a CloseNotify.
● 100	NoRenegotiation	The sender indicates that it cannot comply with the peer's request to renegotiate the TLS handshake; this message is always a warning.

5.4.3   Message Authentication

Another area in which TLS improves on SSL is in the algorithms for message authentication. The way SSL message authentication combines key information and application data is rather ad hoc, created just for the SSL protocol. The TLS protocol, on the other hand, relies on a standard message authentication code known as H-MAC (for Hashed Message Authentication Code). The H-MAC algorithm is a defined standard, and has been subjected to rigorous cryptographic analysis. The H-MAC specification (see the References section) includes a precise description of the approach, as well as sample source code, but figure 5-7 illustrates H-MAC in a format that can be compared with other figures in this text. Note that H-MAC does not specify a particular hash algorithm (such as MD5 or SHA); rather, it works effectively with any competent hash algorithm.

The TLS message authentication code is a straightforward application of the H-MAC standard. The MAC is the result of the H-MAC approach, using whatever hash algorithm the negotiated cipher suite requires. The H-MAC secret is the MAC write secret derived from the master secret. Table 5-4 lists the information that is protected.

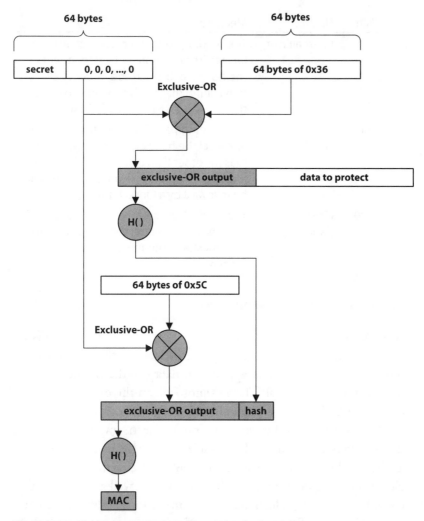

Figure 5-7 Hashed MAC works with any hash algorithm.

Table 5-4 Data Protected by TLS Message Authentication Code

Data Protected by H-MAC

- Sequence number
- TLS protocol message type
- TLS version (e.g., 3.1)
- Message length
- Message contents

5.4.4 Key Material Generation

Building on the H-MAC standard, TLS defines a procedure for using H-MAC to create *pseudorandom output*. This procedure takes a secret value and an initial seed value (which can be quite small), and securely generates random output. The procedure can create as much random output as necessary. Figure 5-8 illustrates the procedure, and table 5-5 lists its steps. As with the H-MAC standard, the procedure does not rely on a particular hash algorithm. Any hash algorithm, including MD5 and SHA may be used for the pseudorandom output.

Table 5-5 Creating Intermediate Pseudorandom Output

Step	Procedure
1	Calculate H-MAC of the secret and the seed.
2	Calculate H-MAC of the secret and the results of the previous step; the result is the first part of the pseudorandom output.
3	Calculate H-MAC of the secret and the results of the previous step; the result is the next part of the pseudorandom output.
4	Repeat step 3 as many times as required to product sufficient pseudorandom output.

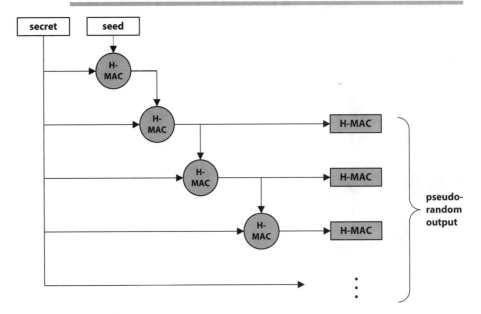

Figure 5-8 TLS uses H-MAC to generate pseudorandom output.

For one additional refinement, TLS uses the pseudorandom output procedure to create a pseudorandom function, or PRF. The PRF combines two separate instances of the pseudorandom output procedure; one uses the MD5 hash algorithm and the other uses the SHA hash algorithm. The TLS standard specifies a function that uses both algorithms just in case one of the two is ever found to be insecure. Should that happen, the other algorithm will still protect the data. The PRF appears in figure 5-9. It starts with a secret value, a seed value, and a label. As the figure shows, the function splits the secret into two parts, one for the MD5 hash and the other for the SHA hash. It also combines the label and the seed into a single value. Table 5-6 lists the detailed steps. Note that the MD5 and SHA hash outputs are of different lengths (16 and 20 bytes, respectively), so the pseudorandom output generation may require a different number of iterations for steps 2 and 3 in the table.

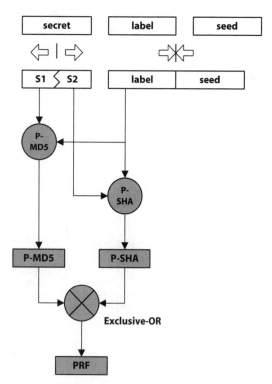

Figure 5-9 TLS's Pseudorandom function uses both MD5 and SHA.

Table 5-6 TLS Pseudorandom Function

Step	Procedure
1	Split the secret into two equal parts; if the secret consists of an odd number of bytes, include the middle byte in each part. (It's the last byte of the first part and the first byte of the second part.)
2	Generate pseudorandom output using the first part of the secret, the MD5 hash function, and the combined label and seed.
3	Generate pseudorandom output using the second part of the secret, the SHA hash function, and the combined label and seed.
4	Exclusive-OR the results from steps 2 and 3.

With an understanding of the TLS PRF, it now possible to describe how TLS creates key material. The principle is the same as with SSL. Each system starts with the premaster secret; next it creates the master secret. Then, it generates the required key material from the master secret. To generate the key material, TLS relies on the PRF. Input values to the PRF are the master secret (as the secret), the ASCII string "key expansion" (as the label), and the concatenation of the server's random value and the client's random value for the seed.

The 48-byte master secret itself is also computed using the PRF. The input values, in this case, are the premaster secret, the ASCII string "master secret" (as the label), and the concatenation of the client's random value and the server's random value. Figure 5-10 illustrates both steps in the process.

5.4.5 CertificateVerify

Transport Layer Security also differs from SSL in the details of the CertificateVerify function. In SSL, the signed information in the CertificateVerify function consists of a complex, two-level hash of handshake messages, master secrets, and padding. (See section 4.5.8.) In the case of TLS, the signed information is simply the handshake messages previously exchanged during the session.

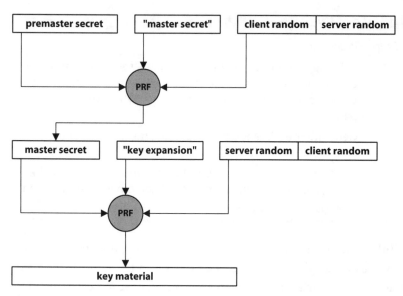

Figure 5-10 TLS uses its PRF to create the master secret and key material.

5.4.6   Finished

The TLS specification also simplifies, slightly, the contents of the Finished message. For TLS, the sole contents of the Finished message are 12 bytes created by applying the PRF to the master secret, the label "client finished" (for clients) or "server finished" (for servers), and the concatenation of the MD5 hash of all handshake messages and the SHA hash of all handshake messages. Figure 5-11 shows the calculation graphically.

5.4.7   Baseline Cipher Suites

As a baseline, TLS supports nearly the same set of cipher suites as SSL; however, explicit support for Fortezza/DMS cipher suites has been removed. The set of defined TLS cipher suites will likely expand as new cipher suites are developed and implemented. Because the IETF has a well-defined process for evaluating these proposals, enhancements will be much easier to add to TLS than they were to SSL. Table 5-7 lists the baseline TLS cipher suites, along with their values in hello messages.

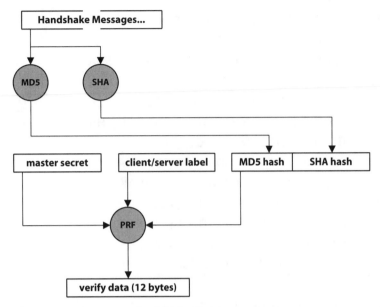

Figure 5-11 TLS uses the PRF for Finished messages.

Table 5-7 TLS Version 1.0 Baseline CipherSuite Values

Value	Cipher Suite
0,0	TLS_NULL_WITH_NULL_NULL
0,1	TLS_RSA_WITH_NULL_MD5
0,2	TLS_RSA_WITH_NULL_SHA
0,3	TLS_RSA_EXPORT_WITH_RC4_40_MD5
0,4	TLS_RSA_WITH_RC4_128_MD5
0,5	TLS_RSA_WITH_RC4_128_SHA
0,6	TLS_RSA_EXPORT_WITH_RC2_CBC_40_MD5
0,7	TLS_RSA_WITH_IDEA_CBC_SHA
0,8	TLS_RSA_EXPORT_WITH_DES40_CBC_SHA
0,9	TLS_RSA_WITH_DES_CBC_SHA
0,10	TLS_RSA_WITH_3DES_EDE_CBC_SHA
0,11	TLS_DH_DSS_EXPORT_WITH_DES40_CBC_SHA
0,12	TLS_DH_DSS_WITH_DES_CBC_SHA
0,13	TLS_DH_DSS_WITH_3DES_EDE_CBC_SHA
0,14	TLS_DH_RSA_EXPORT_WITH_DES40_CBC_SHA

0,15	TLS_DH_RSA_WITH_DES_CBC_SHA
0,16	TLS_DH_RSA_WITH_3DES_EDE_CBC_SHA
0,17	TLS_DHE_DSS_EXPORT_WITH_DES40_CBC_SHA
0,18	TLS_DHE_DSS_WITH_DES_CBC_SHA
0,19	TLS_DHE_DSS_WITH_3DES_EDE_CBC_SHA
0,20	TLS_DHE_RSA_EXPORT_WITH_DES40_CBC_SHA
0,21	TLS_DHE_RSA_WITH_DES_CBC_SHA
0,22	TLS_DHE_RSA_WITH_3DES_EDE_CBC_SHA
0,23	TLS_DH_anon_EXPORT_WITH_RC4_40_MD5
0,24	TLS_DH_anon_WITH_RC4_128_MD5
0,25	TLS_DH_anon_EXPORT_WITH_DES40_CBC_SHA
0,26	TLS_DH_anon_WITH_DES_CBC_SHA
0,27	TLS_DH_anon_WITH_3DES_EDE_CBC_SHA

5.4.8   Interoperability with SSL

As was the case with the transition from SSL version 2.0 to SSL version 3.0, there is a well-defined approach for systems to support both SSL 3.0 and TLS 1.0 in an interoperable manner. Indeed, the process is essentially the same as that described in section 5.1.1. A client that supports both SSL version 3.0 and TLS version 1.0 should send an SSL version 3.0 ClientHello, but with the protocol version set to 3.1. If the server understands TLS, it responds with a TLS ServerHello; otherwise, it responds with an SSL ServerHello, and the client knows to fall back to SSL version 3.0. Servers that support TLS, even if they don't support SSL, should still be prepared to accept an SSL v3.0 ClientHello. If they receive such a message with the version set to 3.1, they can safely proceed with a TLS handshake.

5.5 The Future of SSL and TLS

The future evolution of SSL and TLS is clearly in the hands of the IETF, as well as developers of Web browsers, Web servers, and other Internet systems that require security. Version 3.0 of SSL is well established in these areas, and, as more systems connect to the Internet and more Internet transactions require security, SSL's influence will only grow. Already, devices ranging from WebTV receivers to Palm computers include implementations of SSL or TLS. In addition, applications other than for regular Web commerce are realizing the benefits of an effective network security protocol. The Open Settlement Protocol,[2] for example, relies on SSL to secure IP-based telephony services; and the Wireless Application Protocol Forum has defined a variation of TLS[3] for securing handheld devices.

The shift from SSL as a proprietary technology to TLS as an open standard will also strengthen the protocol. Now that TLS is administered by an international standards organization, participation in its development is open to any interested party. The TLS standardization process gives the network security community much more freedom to improve and enhance the protocol's operation. Should a new vulnerability be discovered, or should new, more effective cryptographic algorithms be developed, it will be much easier to modify TLS appropriately. This benefit alone insures that, under its new name, SSL will continue to secure Internet communications for years to come.

---

[2] Technical Specification TS 101 321 from the European Telecommunications Standards Institute, available at http://www.etsi.org.
[3] The Wireless Transport Layer Security (WTLS) specification is available at http://www.wapforum.org.

Appendix A
X.509 Certificates

The Secure Sockets Layer protocol does not depend on a particular format for the public key certificates it exchanges. As far as SSL is concerned, a certificate is just an arbitrary set of bytes. Practical SSL deployments and implementations, however, depend heavily on the specifics of those certificates. Client implementations, for example, must verify a server's certificate and extract the server's public key information from the certificate in order to encrypt the Client-KeyExchange contents. And, although the SSL protocol itself does not worry about certificate details, a thorough understanding of public key certificates is critical to any SSL implementation.

One particular international standard is widely accepted as the appropriate format for public key certificates. That standard is from the International Telecommunications Union (ITU), and it is universally known by its ITU specification number: X.509. This appendix takes a closer look at the X.509 standard. It begins with an overview of X.509 certificates; the overview provides a high-level description of the certificate format, but it does not include extensive detail. For readers who want to understand X.509 at a detailed level, the following two sections are included. Section A.2 explains *Abstract Syntax Notation One* (ASN.1), a special data description language used extensively in the X.509 (and many other ITU) specifications. Some understanding of ASN.1 is essential for the third section of this appendix, which looks at X.509 certificates in depth. The fourth and final section includes a complete example certificate, which shows how to read the actual certificate byte by byte. This section also discusses important aspects of constructing and interpreting X.509 certificates.

A.1 X.509 Certificate Overview

Certificates that conform to the latest x.509 standard can contain as many as 11 different fields. Their order in the certificate corresponds to the illustration of figure A-1. Note though, that the field names in the figure are *not* the same as the names in the x.509 standard. To this writer, some of the x.509 field names seem quite confusing. Reluctantly, therefore, the figure and the following discussion take the liberty of renaming the fields to more reasonable labels.[1]

A.1.1 Version

The *Version* field identifies the particular version of the x.509 standard to which the certificate conforms. As of this writing, the latest version of the x.509 standard is 3. Note, though, that for this field within the certificate, version numbers begin with 0 rather than 1. Consequently, the version number that appears in x.509 version 3 certificates is 2.

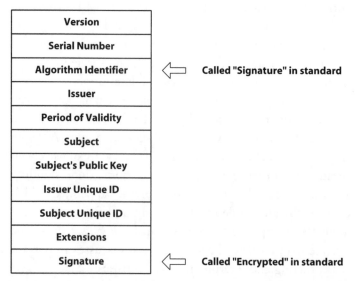

Figure A-1 An X.509 certificate contains fewer than a dozen items.

---

[1] Other authors, including Kaufman, Perlman, and Speciner (see References), have also adopted this approach.

A.1.2 Serial Number

The *Serial Number* is a value assigned by the certificate authority to an individual certificate. Presumably, the CA ensures that the value is unique for every certificate it issues. The certificate authority has complete control over this field, though, and can put any value whatsoever here.

A.1.3 Algorithm Identifier

The *Algorithm Identifier* is one of the fields that is named differently in the standard. The X.509 specification calls this field the *Signature*. That choice is particularly inappropriate, because the field doesn't contain a signature at all. Instead, as the name used here implies, the field simply identifies the algorithm used to sign the certificate, as well as any parameters pertinent to that algorithm. This information is actually repeated in the "encrypted" part of the certificate. Most implementations choose to use the information from that section, effectively ignoring this value.

A.1.4 Issuer

The *Issuer* field identifies the certificate authority that issued the certificate. It takes the form of a *distinguished name*. A distinguished name is a hierarchy, often starting with a country and then dividing into state or province, organizations, organizational units, and so on. Theoretically, a distinguished name may extend all the way to an individual. Certificate authorities have historically been rather liberal in their interpretation of this hierarchy. The organizational unit element, for example, is often used to hold miscellaneous information relating to the authority. The example certificate of section A.4 demonstrates this practice.

A.1.5 Period of Validity

The *Period of Validity* identifies both the earliest and latest times that the certificate is valid. Outside of the bounds this field asserts, the certificate should not be considered valid.

A.1.6 Subject

The *Subject* field identifies the entity that owns the private key being certified. Like the Issuer field, this field takes the form of a distinguished name, and, as with the Issuer, certificate authorities have historically interpreted the distinguished name hierarchy quite liberally. Generally, the most important element in the subject's name is the element known as the *commonName*. The commonName is typically the actual name of the subject being certified.

A.1.7 Subject's Public Key

This field contains the subject's public key, and is, in effect, the whole reason for the certificate. This field also identifies the algorithm and its parameters. As an example, if the public key algorithm is RSA, then this field will contain the modulus and public exponent. Note that this information is different from the information in the Signature and Algorithm Identifier fields of the certificate. Those two fields identify the algorithm of the *certificate authority's* public key, the key used to sign the certificate. This field identifies the *subject's* public key.

A.1.8 Issuer Unique Identifier

This optional field, which was introduced in x.509 version 2, permits two different issuers to have the same *Issuer* distinguished name. Such issuers would be distinguished from each other by having different values for the *Issuer Unique Identifier*. As a practical matter, this field is rarely used.

A.1.9 Subject Unique Identifier

This optional field, also introduced in x.509 version 2, permits two different subjects to have the same distinguished name. For example, two different people in the same organization might be named Stephen Thomas. Such subjects would be distinguished by different values for this field. As a practical matter, like the Issuer Unique Identifier, the Subject Unique Identifier field is rarely used.

A.1.10 Extensions

The *Extensions* field was introduced in version 3 of x.509 (the latest version as of this writing). It provides a place for issuers to add their own private information to the certificate. As discussed in Chapter 5, this is the area where the special object identifiers for Netscape's International Step-Up and Microsoft's Server Gated Cryptography appear. Certificate authorities frequently use this area for miscellaneous information related to the certificate. The sample certificate of section A.4 includes examples of this type of information.

A.1.11 Signature

The *Signature* itself is the final element of an x.509 certificate. As the figure notes, the specification names this field "encrypted." The field contains the algorithm identifier, a secure hash of the other fields in the certificate, and a digital signature of that hash.

A.2 Abstract Syntax Notation One

The x.509 standard describes certificates using a special notation known as *Abstract Syntax One*, or ASN.1 for short. ASN.1 has been called many things (not all of them nice, as it can be a very complex tool), but it resembles, in many respects, a programming language. It is not a true programming language, because ASN.1 really only defines data structures; it cannot effectively describe execution logic. For those familiar with the c programming language, ASN.1 is roughly analogous to the c source code that one typically finds in header (.h) files. It has the equivalent of `structs`, `unions`, `typedefs`, and even `#defines`; ASN.1, however, does not include the equivalent of functions.

Like the c language, ASN.1 has well-defined primitive types, and it has methods to define complex combinations of those primitive types. Those topics, plus the rules for encoding ASN.1 objects for transmission on a network, are the subject of the following subsections. Please note that this entire section contains only the briefest possible introduction to ASN.1. Readers requiring an in-depth discussion of ASN.1 should consult the References section.

A.2.1 Primitive Objects

The ASN.1 specification defines a few key objects as primitive objects. These objects, in fact, are the only objects defined by ASN.1 itself. All other objects are created from combinations of the primitive objects. The ASN.1 primitive objects play the same role that types such as int and char play in the c language. Table A-1 lists some of the ASN.1 primitive objects commonly encountered in x.509 certificates.

Table A-1 Important ASN.1 Primitive Objects

Object	Description
BIT STRING	An array of bits.
BOOLEAN	A value that is either TRUE or FALSE.
IA5String	An OCTET STRING in which the octets are restricted to be valid ASCII characters.
INTEGER	A positive or negative number (ASN.1 INTEGERS have no maximum size).
NULL	An empty object used as a placeholder.
OBJECT IDENTIFIER	A sequence of integers that uniquely identifies a particular object registered (directly or indirectly) with the ITU.
OCTET STRING	An array of bytes (which ASN.1 calls *octets*).
PrintableString	An OCTET STRING in which the octets are restricted to be printable characters.
TeletexString	An OCTET STRING in which the octets are restricted to be characters reproducible by Teletex machines.
UTCTime	A special ASCII string containing a universal time value (popularly known as *Greenwich Mean Time*), in the format YYMMDDHHMMSSZ.

A.2.2 Constructed Objects

The ASN.1 language allows users to build upon its primitive objects by combining them into more complex objects. Just as the c language (to continue the earlier example) allows various combinations such as `struct`, `union`, and arrays, ASN.1 also provides for constructed objects. Table A-2 lists the most common ways to combine ASN.1 primitive types.

Table A-2 Important ASN.1 Constructions

Construct	Description
CHOICE	Exactly one of the following individual objects; corresponds to a C `union`.
SEQUENCE	An *ordered* combination of several individual objects; corresponds to a C `struct`.
SEQUENCE OF	Zero or more of the same individual object (possibly with different values) in which the order of the objects is important; corresponds to a C array, though the size need not be specified.
SET	An *unordered* combination of several individual objects.
SET OF	Zero or more of the same individual object (possibly with different values) in which the order of the objects does not matter.

In X.509 certificates, the only constructions that commonly appear are SEQUENCE, SET, and CHOICE. The example certificate of section A.4 includes examples of both types.

A.2.3 The Object Identifier Hierarchy

The OBJECT IDENTIFIER primitive type is a special feature of ASN.1 that is not part of standard programming languages such as C. An OBJECT IDENTIFIER value refers to a specific place in a special hierarchy of objects. Every object within this hierarchy has its own unique OBJECT IDENTIFIER value, and, with only this value, it is possible to unambiguously identify the corresponding object.

The ITU has defined an initial hierarchy for these objects. In graphical form, the object hierarchy looks like figure A-2. At the highest level, the hierarchy recognizes the ITU, the International Standards Organization (ISO), and joint ITU-ISO objects. Many other public and

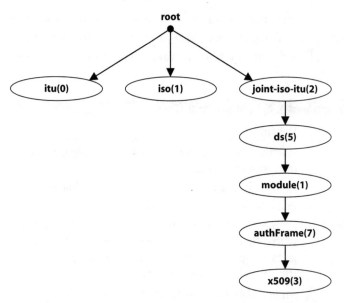

Figure A-2 OBJECT IDENTIFIER values are organized as a hierarchy.

private organizations (including, for example, the IETF, the European Telecommunications Standards Institute, and others) have their own object hierarchies beneath one of the three top-level organizations.

The figure details one example hierarchy under the joint ITU/ISO subtree. That hierarchy consists of directory services (ds), modules, an authentication framework, and, finally, x.509. This is the main path for x.509 objects.

As you can see, the OBJECT IDENTIFIER hierarchy is a little like the Internet's domain name system (DNS). In that system, the domain name www.ibm.com refers (reading backward) to commercial organizations in general (.com), then a particular company (ibm), and then a specific system belonging to that company (www.). Borrowing from the DNS tradition, OBJECT IDENTIFIER values may be written using a dot notation. A period separates different levels of the hierarchy. Unlike domain names, OBJECT IDENTIFIER values are normally written from most general to most specific. Furthermore, levels in the OBJECT IDENTIFIER hierarchy are represented by numbers rather than names. The x.509 branch from the tree above, therefore, commonly appears as 2.5.1.7.3.

A.2.4 Tagging

Another unique ASN.1 characteristic is tagging. A tag associates a unique value with a specific ASN.1 object or element within an object. This function sounds similar to that of an OBJECT IDENTIFIER, but the two concepts are really quite different. The OBJECT IDENTIFIER hierarchy is a global, distributed hierarchy that is actually independent of the ASN.1 language. The ASN.1 language happens to have a native, primitive type that represents OBJECT IDENTIFIER values, but other languages could support the OBJECT IDENTIFIER hierarchy equally well. Tags, on the other hand, are an intimate and essential part of ASN.1. The ASN.1 language has greater flexibility than many data description languages, and tags are one of the essential tools ASN.1 needs to support that flexibility.

The easiest way to sort this out is with an example, so let's take a look at some samples of ASN.1. Table A-3 shows an ASN.1 description of a complex object. The example object (which is somewhat artificial in order to clarify the important concepts) has two optional components and one printable string. The two optional components are both OBJECT IDENTIFIER values, and they could be used to indicate the governmental level of a location. The ITU, for example, has defined OBJECT IDENTIFIER values for country, state or province, and locality, and either of these components could indicate whether the location is a country, state, city, or other. The important thing to note is that the sample ASN.1 defines both the primaryLevel and the secondaryLevel to be OPTIONAL. That means that a Location object could have both, neither, or one or the other of these elements.

Table A-3 Tagging within an Object

ASN.1 Source
Location ::= SEQUENCE {
primaryLevel   [0] OBJECT IDENTIFIER OPTIONAL,
secondaryLevel [1] OBJECT IDENTIFIER OPTIONAL,
placeName   PrintableString }

Now, consider how to interpret a Location instance that contains only a single element of type OBJECT IDENTIFIER. Perhaps the Location has an OBJECT IDENTIFIER value of 2.5.4.6, which the ITU defines to be "country." Does this OBJECT IDENTIFIER value mean that the location's primary level is a country; or is it the secondary level that's the country? The answer lies in the bracketed numbers immediately before each OBJECT IDENTIFIER keyword. Those numbers are tags. All primaryLevel elements will have a tag value of 0, and secondary-Level elements have a tag of 1. Any valid Location instance will include the appropriate tag value along with the OBJECT IDENTIFIER value. A quick check of the tag value is enough to tell which OBJECT IDENTIFIER is present in the Location object.

To summarize, the OBJECT IDENTIFIER hierarchy is a globally administered way to unambiguously refer to any object, and ASN.1 happens to have some built-in features that make working with the hierarchy easy. Tags, on the other hand, are an integral part of ASN.1 and are used to distinguish particular ASN.1 objects or elements from each other.

The previous example is only one way that tags distinguish ASN.1 objects from each other. The language actually has four different types of tags: universal, application-specific, context-specific, and private-use. What we've been discussing so far are context-specific tags. The 0 and 1 of table A-3 only have meaning in the context of a Location object. Different objects could safely reuse these tag values without the risk of confusion.

Two of the other types of tags—application-specific and private-use—are rarely used in any ASN.1, and are not relevant to X.509 certificates, so we won't discuss them further here. Universal tags, on the other hand, are important. They are used to distinguish between ASN.1's primitive types and constructed objects. The ASN.1 standards define specific universal tag values for all the primitive types and construction operations. Table A-4 lists some that are important for X.509 certificates. Note that universal tags have the same numeric values as context-specific tags. (The universal tag for a BOOLEAN object is the same value, 1, as the context-specific tag for secondaryLevel OBJECT IDENTIFIER values in the previous example.) That's not really a problem, though. As we'll see, ASN.1 has ways to indicate whether a particular tag is universal or context-specific.

Table A-4 ASN.1 Universal Tags

Universal Tag	ASN.1 Object
1	BOOLEAN
2	INTEGER
3	BIT STRING
4	OCTET STRING
5	NULL
6	OBJECT IDENTIFIER
16	SEQUENCE, SEQUENCE OF
17	SET, SET OF
19	PrintableString
20	TeletexString
22	IA5String
23	UTCTime

In addition to belonging to a class, tags are either IMPLICIT or EXPLICIT. By default, all tags are explicit, so the OBJECT IDENTIFIER elements of Location objects are both explicitly tagged. That means that all primaryLevel elements will have two separate tags. The first is a context-specific tag of 0 just described; the second is a universal tag of 6, indicating an OBJECT IDENTIFIER. Most of the time, the second tag is not necessary. In our example, by identifying the element as primaryLevel, the context-specific tag alone also implies that the element is an OBJECT IDENTIFIER. The universal tag that indicates the element is an OBJECT IDENTIFIER value is unnecessary. This idea leads to the ASN.1 of table A-5. The IMPLICIT keyword with each element indicates that the second tag for the type itself is not needed. So, if Location is defined as in table A-5, a primaryLevel element will only have a single tag, the context-specific tag of 0. The universal tag for OBJECT IDENTIFIER is merely implied and not actually present.

Table A-5 Marking Tags as Implicit

ASN.1 Source
Location ::= SEQUENCE {
primaryLevel   [0] IMPLICIT OBJECT IDENTIFIER OPTIONAL,
secondaryLevel [1] IMPLICIT OBJECT IDENTIFIER OPTIONAL,
placeName   PrintableString }

A.2.5   Encoding Rules

When ASN.1 is used to define actual objects that are transferred across a communications network, it must be possible to represent those objects to computers. Representing ASN.1 objects is known as *encoding*, and ASN.1 defines several different approaches. For X.509 certificates, the approach is that of the *Distinguished Encoding Rules*, or DER for short.

The Distinguished Encoding Rules for ASN.1 are relatively straightforward. Nearly all objects consist of the three parts that figure A-3 shows: a tag, a length, and a value. (DER also has a method of encoding objects whose final length is unknown when the encoding process begins, but this method doesn't apply to X.509 certificates.)

The first part of any encoded object is the object's tag. Tags are encoded in one of two ways, depending on whether their numeric value is less than 31. Figure A-4 shows how tag values less than 31 are encoded. The two most significant bits indicate the class of the tag; table A-6 spells out their values. The next bit indicates whether the object is primitive or constructed, and the five least significant bits carry the tag value itself. For example, the tag for SEQUENCE is encoded as a hexadecimal 0x30. The class bits 00 indicate a universal tag. The next bit is a 1 to indicate that the object is constructed, and the five remaining bits are 10000 for the universal tag of 16.

Table A-6 Class Encoding Bit Values for Tags

Bits	Class
0 0	Universal Tag
0 1	Application-Specific Tag
1 0	Context-Specific Tag
1 1	Private-Use Tag

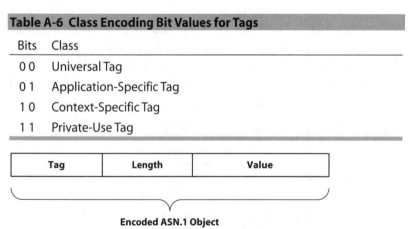

Encoded ASN.1 Object

Figure A-3 ASN.1 encodes objects as a tag, a length, and a value.

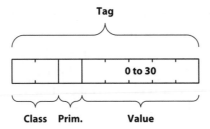

Figure A-4 Small tag values are encoded as a single byte.

When the tag value is greater than 30, the format shown in the bottom of figure A-5 encodes the tag. The class and primitive bits are the same as before, but the five least significant bits of the first byte are all ones. The value itself is present in the subsequent bytes. The most significant bit of these bytes is the *extension* bit. This extension bit is set to 1 in all bytes but the last. The remaining bits, when concatenated together, form the complete tag value. There is no theoretical limit to the number of bytes DER uses to encode tag values, so DER can successfully encode arbitrarily large tag values.

The length component of each object follows a similar (but not identical) strategy. If the length is less than 128, it is encoded as a single byte with a value equal to the length. For objects greater than 127 bytes in length, the most significant bit of the first byte is set to 1, and the rest of that byte indicates the number of bytes in the length. The length itself then follows. For example, a length of 100 000 bytes appears as the hexadecimal value 0x830186A0. The first byte (0x83) indicates that the length is greater than 127, and that it is present in the next 3 bytes. Those bytes (0x0186A0, which is the hexadecimal representation of 100 000) hold the value itself.

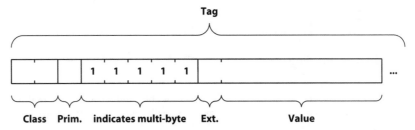

Figure A-5 Tag values greater than 30 use a multi-byte encoding.

The encoding of the object's value depends on the object's type, but the process is relatively straightforward. String objects such as OCTET STRING, IA5string, and UTCtime simply encode the individual bytes of the string. The INTEGER object uses two's complement binary notation, while BIT STRING objects are encoded like OCTET STRING objects, except that the first byte after the length contains the number of unused bits in the final byte.

The only primitive type with a tricky encoding is the OBJECT IDENTIFIER. For an OBJECT IDENTIFIER, the encoding rules are sufficiently complicated that they are best explained by an example. Figure A-6 shows the steps involved in encoding the OBJECT IDENTIFIER value 1.0.8571.2. The first step combines the first two components of the value (the 1 and the 0) by multiplying the first by 40 and adding the second.[2] Then each of the resulting components is converted to a binary value, which is, in turn, grouped into 7-bit quantities. Each of these 7-bit quantities becomes a single byte in the encoding. The most significant bit of each byte is set to 0 on the last 7-bit quantity

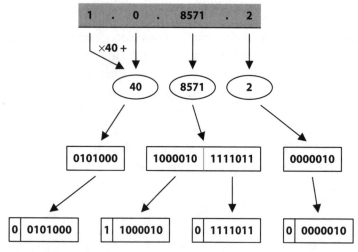

Figure A-6 Encoding OBJECT IDENTIFIER values takes several steps.

---

[2] The ASN.1 designers had a reason for this approach, but, in hindsight, the resulting complexity and political repercussions would probably cause them to reconsider if they could. What's done is done, however.

of each component, and it is set to 1 on all other bytes. The final encoding of the OBJECT IDENTIFIER value 1.0.8571.2 is 0x28C27B02.

Constructed objects defined as a SEQUENCE and SET use the tag for the appropriate construction, the length of the entire construction, and then normal DER encodings of the individual objects within the construction. Again, an actual example such as that of section A.4 provides the best illustration of such encodings.

A.3 X.509 Certificate Definition

Although the X.509 specification contains more than 70 pages, the essential definition of an X.509 certificate consists of only 45 lines of ASN.1 source code that define 10 objects. This section examines each of those major objects.

A.3.1 The Certificate Object

The primary object for an X.509 certificate is the Certificate object itself. Table A-7 shows the 14 lines of ASN.1 that make up its definition. Line 1 highlights two key aspects of the Certificate object. First, it is digitally signed. The SIGNED construction is an ASN.1 *parameterized type*, essentially the same as a C-language macro. In this case, it indicates that the information to be signed (the ASN.1 SEQUENCE that follows) is itself followed by an AlgorithmIdentifier, then by the BIT STRING containing the results of the signing algorithm.

Table A-7 X.509 Certificate Object

Line	ASN.1 Source	
1	Certificate ::= SIGNED { SEQUENCE {	
2	version	[0] Version DEFAULT v1,
3	serialNumber	CertificateSerialNumber,
4	signature	AlgorithmIdentifier,
5	issuer	Name,
6	validity	Validity,
7	subject	Name,
8	subjectPublicKeyInfo	SubjectPublicKeyInfo,
9	issuerUniqueIdentifier	[1] IMPLICIT UniqueIdentifier OPTIONAL,

Line	ASN.1 Source	
10	-- if present, version must be v2 or v3	
11	subjectUniqueIdentifier	[2] IMPLICIT UniqueIdentifier OP-TIONAL,
12	-- if present, version must be v2 or v3	
13	extensions	[3] Extensions OPTIONAL
14	-- If present, version must be v3 -- } }	

Line 1 also shows that the Certificate object is a SEQUENCE of other objects. Those other objects are defined by lines 2 through 14 of the ASN.1; each is discussed in following subsections. Note also that lines 10, 12, and 14 begin with a double dash, or --. This is the ASN.1 notation for a comment. Comments continue to the end of the line, or, as in line 14, until another double dash is encountered.

Most of the components of a Certificate object are a straightforward application of their respective objects, and thus are discussed in the following subsections. The "signature" component in line 4, however, is a bit tricky. It merely identifies the signature algorithm that the issuer uses to sign the certificate; it is not actually a signature for the certificate. Its value is also repeated as part of the SIGNED construction, although that second occurrence is not included in the data being signed. Because of this repetition, and because the AlgorithmIdentifier object has historically been the subject of considerable confusion, many implementations simply ignore this field in the certificate, and instead rely on the value in the SIGNED construction.

A.3.2   The Version Object

The Version object identifies which version of the x.509 standard the certificate complies with. As table A-8 indicates, the object is a simple INTEGER. It takes on the values 0, 1, or 2—for version 1, 2, or 3 of x.509, respectively.

Table A-8 X.509 Version Object

Line	ASN.1 Source
15	Version := INTEGER { v1(0), v2(1), v3(2) }

A.3.3   The CertificateSerialNumber Object

The CertificateSerialNumber is, as table A-9 shows, an INTEGER.

Line	ASN.1 Source
Table A-9 X.509 CertificateSerialNumber Object	
16	CertificateSerialNumber ::= INTEGER

A.3.4   The AlgorithmIdentifier Object

The AlgorithmIdentifier object has caused a lot of confusion for SSL implementations. Part of the reason is that, as table A-10 shows, the X.509 specification does not fully define the object. Rather, it provides a framework for defining AlgorithmIdentifier objects, and leaves the messy details up to other specifications. That has left the door open for many different bodies, including the ITU, the IETF, industry consortia, and proprietary vendors, to devise their own algorithm identifiers. What makes the situation particularly frustrating is that there really aren't that many practical algorithms; the result has been many different ways to refer to the same few algorithms.

Line	ASN.1 Source
Table A-10 X.509 AlgorithmIdentifier Object	
17	AlgorithmIdentifier ::= SEQUENCE {
18	algorithm ALGORITHM.&id ({SupportedAlgorithms}),
19	parameters ALGORITHM.&Type ({SupportedAlgorithms}{ @algorithm}) OPTIONAL }
20	-- Definition of the following information object set is deferred, perhaps to standardized
21	-- profiles or to protocol implementation conformance statements. The set is required to
22	-- specify a table constraint on the parameters component of AlgorithmIdentifier
23	-- SupportedAlgorithms ALGORITHM ::= { ... }

Fortunately in this case, the void left by de jure standards has been filled by de facto implementations. The majority of existing SSL implementations rely on certificates issued by VeriSign or one of its partners. And VeriSign is generally consistent in using the following two algorithm identifiers. For public keys, the OBJECT IDENTIFIER (1 2 840 113549 1 1 1) indicates RSA public key encryption. And for digital signatures, the OBJECT IDENTIFIER (1 2 840 113549 1 1 4) represents the combination of MD5 hash and RSA signing. The sample certificate of section A.4 includes examples of both AlgorithmIdentifier objects. Issuers other than VeriSign are likely to use the same identifiers to ensure interoperability with existing implementations.

A.3.5   The Validity Object

The Validity object, whose definition appears in table A-11, is a SEQUENCE of two times. The first is the *notBefore* time; the certificate should not be considered valid until that time is reached. The second element of the SEQUENCE is the *notAfter* time. This is the expiration time for the certificate. Section A.3.7 below shows the definition of each time value.

Table A-11 X.509 Validity Object

Line	ASN.1 Source
24	Validity ::= SEQUENCE {
25	notBefore Time,
26	notAfter Time }

A.3.6   The SubjectPublicKeyInfo Object

The subject's public key information is carried within a SubjectPublicKeyInfo object. As table A-12 shows, that object contains an AlgorithmIdentifier, followed by the public key itself.

Table A-12 X.509 SubjectPublicKeyInfo Object

Line	ASN.1 Source	
27	SubjectPublicKeyInfo ::= SEQUENCE {	
28	algorithm	AlgorithmIdentifier,
29	subjectPublicKey	BIT STRING }

A.3.7 The Time Object

Table A-13 shows how a Time object can be described in either of two formats: as a universal time string or as a generalized time string. Nearly all implementations choose the universal time string alternative.

Table A-13 X.509 Time Object

Line	ASN.1 Source	
30	Time ::= CHOICE {	
31	utcTime	UTCTime,
32	generalizedTime	GeneralizedTime }

A.3.8 The Extensions Object

The X.509 Extensions object is, as table A-14 indicates, a sequence of one or more individual Extension objects. (Note the change from plural to singular.) Each Extension consists of an identifier, an indication of whether the particular extension is critical, and the extension value. The *critical* element assists systems that receive a certificate with extensions they do not understand. If the critical element is FALSE, then those systems can simply ignore the extensions they cannot interpret. An extension that is critical, however, should not be ignored. A system that doesn't understand a critical extension should play it safe and treat the entire certificate as invalid.

Table A-14 X.509 Extensions

Line	ASN.1 Source	
33	Extensions	::= SEQUENCE OF Extension
34	Extension	::= SEQUENCE {
35	extnId	EXTENSION.&id ({ExtensionSet}),
36	critical	BOOLEAN DEFAULT FALSE,
37	extnValue	OCTET STRING
38		-- *contains a* DER *encoding of a value of type &ExtnType*
39		-- *for the extension object identified by extnId* -- }

Two particular extensions that are important to SSL are the extended key usage extensions that indicate International Step-Up and Server

Gated Cryptography. (See sections 5.2 and 5.3.) Currently, any certificate that supports International Step-Up also supports Server Gated Cryptography. Such certificates include both extensions. The extKeyUsage OBJECT IDENTIFIER is (2 5 29 37), and its value, in this case, consists of the sequence of OBJECT IDENTIFIER values (2 16 840 1 113730 4 1) and (1 3 6 1 4 1 311 10 3 3). The example certificate of section A.4 shows this extension in full context.

A.3.9   The UniqueIdentifier Object

The X.509 certificate includes a few objects that are not defined in the X.509 specification itself, but are instead found in other ITU recommendations. The UniqueIdentifier object is one of those externally defined objects. For completeness, table A-15 shows its definition. Note that a UniqueIdentifier is simply an arbitrary bit string.

Table A-15 X.500 UniqueIdentifier Object

Line	ASN.1 Source
40	UniqueIdentifier ::= BIT STRING

A.3.10 The Name Object

A more significant object defined outside of the X.509 specification is the Name object. Names are used to identify both subjects and issuers of certificates. As table A-16 shows, a Name is a series of RelativeDistinguishedName objects, where each of these objects is a set of one or more attributes.

Table A-16 X.500 Name Object

Line	ASN.1 Source	
41	Name ::= SEQUENCE OF RelativeDistinguishedName	
42	RelativeDistinguishedName ::= SET OF AttributeValueAssertion	
43	AttributeValueAssertion ::= SEQUENCE {	
44	attributeType	OBJECT IDENTIFIER
45	attributeValue	ANY }

The important organizing concept behind Name objects is a hierarchy. An example makes this clearer. I live in the town of Marietta. That information alone, though, is not really enough to identify my current hometown. There are at least 11 different cities in the United States alone named Marietta. A complete identification would be the town of Marietta, the state of Georgia, and the country of the United States.

Figure A-7 shows this organization graphically. In X.509 terms, the Name for my town would be something like country=US, state=GA, city=Marietta. That full name consists of three separate RelativeDistinguishedName objects: country=US, state=GA, and city=Marietta. To take the last of these RelativeDistinguishedName objects, it is a single AttributeValueAssertion where the attributeType is city and the attributeValue is Marietta.

Of course, certificates are not normally issued to or by cities. They typically identify a person or an organization, frequently in a business context. Various official and unofficial standards define many different attributes that can appear in an X.509 certificate. Table A-17 lists some of the more common ones. Each type in the list consists of an OBJECT IDENTIFIER and an object for its value.

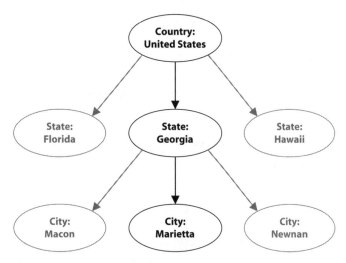

Figure A-7 Distinguished names are organized in a hierarchy.

Table A-17 Typical X.509 Name Attribute Types

Attribute	ASN.1 Description
countryName ::=	SEQUENCE { { 2 5 4 6 }, StringType(SIZE(2)) }
organization ::=	SEQUENCE { { 2 5 4 10 }, StringType(SIZE(1...64)) }
organizationalUnitName ::=	SEQUENCE { { 2 5 4 11 }, StringType(SIZE(1...64)) }
commonName ::=	SEQUENCE { { 2 5 4 3 }, StringType(SIZE(1...64)) }
localityName ::=	SEQUENCE { { 2 5 4 7 }, StringType(SIZE(1...64)) }
stateOrProvinceName ::=	SEQUENCE { { 2 5 4 8 }, StringType(SIZE(1...64)) }
emailAddress ::=	SEQUENCE { { 1 2 840 113549 1 9 1 }, IA5String }

A.4 Example Certificate

Although descriptions of ASN.1 and X.509 certificates can be helpful, full understanding comes from actually looking at a real certificate. This section presents a complete X.509 certificate actually used for SSL security. Table A-18 shows the full certificate, matching the encoded bytes with the appropriate ASN.1 source. The leftmost column in the table indicates the offset (in hexadecimal) from the beginning of the certificate. This value is important, as further discussion in this section refers to specific components of the certificate by reference to their offset.

Table A-18 Example X.509 Certificate

Offset	Certificate Contents	ASN.1
0000	30 82 05 64	SEQUENCE, len=0x564
	30 82 04 CD	SEQUENCE, len=0x4CD
	A0 03	EXPLICIT TAG [0], len=3
	02 01	INTEGER, len=1
	02	2
	02 10	INTEGER, len=0x10

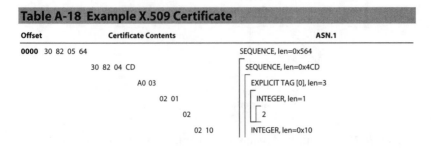

Offset	Certificate Contents	ASN.1
	3E	value=0x3E29...
0010	29 CF 54 69 08 2B 0F AB 73 2D 95 39 A5 97 2C	
	30	SEQUENCE, len=0xD
0020	0D	
	06 09	OBJECT IDENTIFIER, len=9
	2A 86 48 86 F7 0D 01 01 04	1.2.840.113549.1.1.4
	05 00	NULL, len=0
	30 81	SEQUENCE, len=0xBA
0030	BA	
	31 1F	SET, len=0x1F
	30 1D	SEQUENCE, len=0x1D
	06 03	OBJECT IDENTIFIER, len=3
	55 04 0A	2.5.4.10
	13 16	PrintableString, len=0x16
	56 65 72 69	"VeriSign Trust Network"
0040	53 69 67 6E 20 54 72 75 73 74 20 4E 65 74 77 6F	
0050	72 6B	
	31 17	SET, len=0x17
	30 15	SEQUENCE, len=0x15
	06 03	OBJECT IDENTIFIER, len=3
	55 04 0B	2.5.4.11
	13 0E	PrintableString, len=0xE
	56 65 72	"VeriSign, Inc."
0060	69 53 69 67 6E 2C 20 49 6E 63 2E	
	31 33	SET, len=0x33
	30 31	SEQUENCE, len=0x31
	06	OBJECT IDENTIFIER, len=3
0070	03	
	55 04 0B	2.5.4.11
	13 2A	PrintableString, len=0x2A
	56 65 72 69 53 69 67 6E 20 49	"VeriSign International
0080	6E 74 65 72 6E 61 74 69 6F 6E 61 6C 20 53 65 72	Server CA = Class 3"
0090	76 65 72 20 43 41 20 2D 20 43 6C 61 73 73 20 33	
00A0	31 49	SET, len=0x49
	30 47	SEQUENCE, len=0x47
	06 03	OBJECT IDENTIFIER, len=3
	55 04 0B	2.5.4.11
	13 40	PrintableString, len=0x40
	77 77 77 2E 76	"www.verisign.com/CPS
00B0	65 72 69 73 69 67 6E 2E 63 6F 6D 2F 43 50 53 20	Incorp.by Ref.
00C0	49 6E 63 6F 72 70 2E 62 79 20 52 65 66 2E 20 4C	LIABILITY LTD.(c)97
00D0	49 41 42 49 4C 49 54 59 20 4C 54 44 2E 28 63 29	VeriSign"
00E0	39 37 20 56 65 72 69 53 69 67 6E	

Offset	Certificate Contents	ASN.1
	30 1E	SEQUENCE, len=0x1E
	17 0D	UTCTime, len=0xD
	39	"981203000000Z"
00F0	38 31 32 30 33 30 30 30 30 30 5A	
	17 0D	UTCTime, len=0xD
	39 39	"991211235959Z"
0100	31 32 31 31 32 33 35 39 35 39 5A	
	30 81 89	SEQUENCE, len=0x89
	31 0B	SET, len=0xB
0110	30 09	SEQUENCE, len=9
	06 03	OBJECT IDENTIFIER, len=3
	55 04 06	2.5.4.6
	13 02	PrintableString, len=2
	4E 5A	"NZ"
	31 11	SET, len=0x11
	30 0F	SEQUENCE, len=0xF
	06	OBJECT IDENTIFIER, len=3
0120	03	
	55 04 08	2.5.4.8
	13 08	PrintableString, len=8
	41 75 63 6B 6C 61 6E 64	"Auckland"
	31 11	SET, len=0x11
0130	30 0F	SEQUENCE, len=0xF
	06 03	OBJECT IDENTIFIER, len=3
	55 04 07	2.5.4.7
	14 08	TeletexString, len=8
	41 75 63 6B 6C 61 6E	"Auckland"
0140	64	
	31 19	SET, len=0x19
	30 17	SEQUENCE, len=0x17
	06 03	OBJECT IDENTIFIER, len=3
	55 04 0A	2.5.4.10
	14 10	TeletexString, len=0x10
	41 53 42 20	"ASB Bank Limited"
0150	42 61 6E 6B 20 4C 69 6D 69 74 65 64	
	31 1D	SET, len=0x1D
	30 1B	SEQUENCE, len=0x1B
0160	06 03	OBJECT IDENTIFIER, len=3
	55 04 0B	2.5.4.11
	14 14	TeletexString, len=0x14
	49 6E 66 6F 72 6D 61 74 69	"Information Services"
0170	6F 6E 20 53 65 72 76 69 63 65 73	
	31 1A	SET, len=0x1A

Offset	Certificate Contents	ASN.1
	30 18	SEQUENCE, len=0x18
	06	OBJECT IDENTIFIER, len=3
0180 03		
	55 04 03	2.5.4.3
	14 11	TeletexString, len=0x11
	77 77 77 2E 61 73 62 62 61 6E	"www.asbbank.co.nz"
0190 6B 2E 63 6F 2E 6E 7A		
	30 81 9E	SEQUENCE, len=0x9E
	30 0D	SEQUENCE, len=0xD
	06 09	OBJECT IDENTIFIER, len=9
	2A 86	1.2.840.113549.1.1.1
01A0 48 86 F7 0D 01 01 01		
	05 00	NULL, len=0
	03 81 8C 00	BIT STRING, len=0x8C, unused=0
	30 81 88	0x308188...
01B0 02 81 80 6C BE 1F AF 40 43 3F 8C B9 77 77 40 16		
01C0 9A CF C7 5B 9B E9 5F D8 E5 2E A0 CC A5 85 09 F6		
01D0 67 27 EC C9 78 BF 74 96 B0 38 6C C6 93 C4 62 82		
01E0 F8 3B 84 EB 82 1D 48 C3 2A 68 C3 08 D5 6B E3 55		
01F0 2C AA A3 8B 81 EE 77 17 12 0A F0 03 CE CE A6 14		
0200 DF AB EC E0 C4 B4 77 8B 97 88 A3 12 29 A2 36 A2		
0210 9E F9 66 A0 5E 8E FD 6D FB 83 51 41 C9 0B F8 7B		
0220 E4 15 13 D9 C8 8D 2C 83 1A A6 CE 6A A4 90 FD 11		
0230 25 86 73 02 03 01 00 01		
	A3 82 02 99	EXPLICIT TAG [3], len=0x299
	30 82 02 95	SEQUENCE, len=0x295
0240 30 09		SEQUENCE, len=9
	06 03	OBJECT IDENTIFER, len=3
	55 1D 13	2.5.29.19
	04 02	OCTET STRING, len=2
	30 00	*SEQUENCE, len=0*
	30 82 02 1F	SEQUENCE, len=0x21F
	06	OBJECT IDENTIFIER, len=3
0250 03		
	55 1D 03	2.5.29.3
	04 82 02 16	OCTET STRING, len=0x216
	30 82 02 12	*SEQUENCE, len=0x212*
	30 82 02 0E	SEQUENCE, len=0x20E
0260 30 82 02 0A		SEQUENCE, len=0x20A
	06 0B	OBJECT ID., len=0xB
	60 86 48 01 86 F8 45 01 07 01	2.16.840.1.113733.1.7.1.1
0270 01		
	30 82 01 F9	SEQUENCE, len=0x1F9

Offset	Certificate Contents	ASN.1
	16 82 01 A7	IA5String, len=0x1A7
	54 68 69 73 20 63 65	"This certificate
0280	72 74 69 66 69 63 61 74 65 20 69 6E 63 6F 72 70	incorporates by
0290	6F 72 61 74 65 73 20 62 79 20 72 65 66 65 72 65	reference, and its
02A0	6E 63 65 2C 20 61 6E 64 20 69 74 73 20 75 73 65	use is strictly
02B0	20 69 73 20 73 74 72 69 63 74 6C 79 20 73 75 62	subject to, the
02C0	6A 65 63 74 20 74 6F 2C 20 74 68 65 20 56 65 72	VeriSign Certification
02D0	69 53 69 67 6E 20 43 65 72 74 69 66 69 63 61 74	Practice Statement
02E0	69 6F 6E 20 50 72 61 63 74 69 63 65 20 53 74 61	(CPS), available at:
02F0	74 65 6D 65 6E 74 20 28 43 50 53 29 2C 20 61 76	https://www.verisign
0300	61 69 6C 61 62 6C 65 20 61 74 3A 20 68 74 74 70	.com /CPS; by E-mail at
0310	73 3A 2F 2F 77 77 77 2E 76 65 72 69 73 69 67 6E	CPS-requests@verisign.
0320	2E 63 6F 6D 2F 43 50 53 3B 20 62 79 20 45 2D 6D	com; or by mail at
0330	61 69 6C 20 61 74 20 43 50 53 2D 72 65 71 75 65	VeriSign, Inc., 2593
0340	73 74 73 40 76 65 72 69 73 69 67 6E 2E 63 6F 6D	Coast Ave., Mountain
0350	3B 20 6F 72 20 62 79 20 6D 61 69 6C 20 61 74 20	View, CA 94043 USA
0360	56 65 72 69 53 69 67 6E 2C 20 49 6E 63 2E 2C 20	Tel. +1 (415) 961-8830
0370	32 35 39 33 20 43 6F 61 73 74 20 41 76 65 2E 2C	Copyright (c) 1996
0380	20 4D 6F 75 6E 74 61 69 6E 20 56 69 65 77 2C 20	VeriSign, Inc All Rights
0390	43 41 20 39 34 30 34 33 20 55 53 41 20 54 65 6C	Reserved. CERTAIN
03A0	2E 20 2B 31 20 28 34 31 35 29 20 39 36 31 2D 38	WARRANTIES
03B0	38 33 30 20 43 6F 70 79 72 69 67 68 74 20 28 63	DISCLAIMED and
03C0	29 20 31 39 39 36 20 56 65 72 69 53 69 67 6E 2C	LIABILITY LIMITED."
03D0	20 49 6E 63 2E 20 20 41 6C 6C 20 52 69 67 68 74	
03E0	73 20 52 65 73 65 72 76 65 64 2E 20 43 45 52 54	
03F0	41 49 4E 20 57 41 52 52 41 4E 54 49 45 53 20 44	
0400	49 53 43 4C 41 49 4D 45 44 20 61 6E 64 20 4C 49	
0410	41 42 49 4C 49 54 59 20 4C 49 4D 49 54 45 44 2E	
0420	A0 0E	TAG [0], len=0xE
	06 0C	OBJECT ID., len=0xC
	60 86 48 01 86 F8 45 01 07 01 01 01	2.16.840.1.113733.1.7.1.1.1
0430	A1 0E	TAG [1], len=0xE
	06 0C	OBJECT ID. len=0xC
	60 86 48 01 86 F8 45 01 07 01 01 02	2.16.840.1.113733.1.7.1.1.2
0440	30 2C	SEQUENCE, len=0x2C
	30 2A	SEQUENCE, len=0x2A
	16 28	IA5String, len=0x28
	68 74 74 70 73 3A 2F 2F 77 77	"https://www.
0450	77 2E 76 65 72 69 73 69 67 6E 2E 63 6F 6D 2F 72	verisign.com
0460	65 70 6F 73 69 74 6F 72 79 2F 43 50 53 20	/repository/CPS "
	30 11	SEQUENCE, len=0x11
0470	06 09	OBJECT IDENTIFIER, len=9
	60 86 48 01 86 F8 42 01 01	2.16.840.1.113730.1.1
	04 04	OCTET STRING, len=4

Offset	Certificate Contents	ASN.1

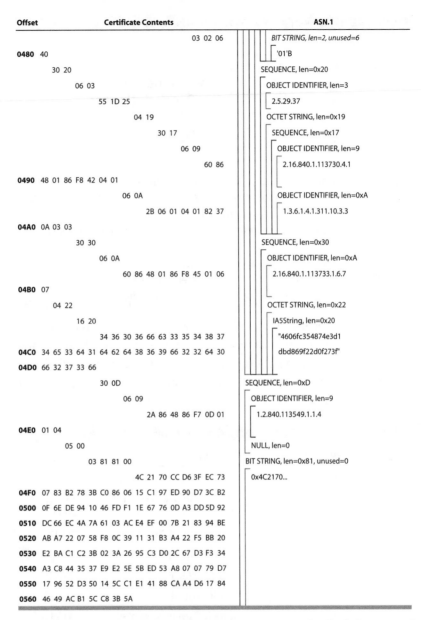

	03 02 06	*BIT STRING, len=2, unused=6*
0480 40		'01'B
30 20		SEQUENCE, len=0x20
06 03		OBJECT IDENTIFIER, len=3
55 1D 25		2.5.29.37
04 19		OCTET STRING, len=0x19
30 17		SEQUENCE, len=0x17
06 09		OBJECT IDENTIFIER, len=9
60 86		2.16.840.1.113730.4.1
0490 48 01 86 F8 42 04 01		
06 0A		OBJECT IDENTIFIER, len=0xA
2B 06 01 04 01 82 37		1.3.6.1.4.1.311.10.3.3
04A0 0A 03 03		
30 30		SEQUENCE, len=0x30
06 0A		OBJECT IDENTIFIER, len=0xA
60 86 48 01 86 F8 45 01 06		2.16.840.1.113733.1.6.7
04B0 07		
04 22		OCTET STRING, len=0x22
16 20		IA5String, len=0x20
34 36 30 36 66 63 33 35 34 38 37		"4606fc354874e3d1
04C0 34 65 33 64 31 64 62 64 38 36 39 66 32 32 64 30		dbd869f22d0f273f"
04D0 66 32 37 33 66		
30 0D		SEQUENCE, len=0xD
06 09		OBJECT IDENTIFIER, len=9
2A 86 48 86 F7 0D 01		1.2.840.113549.1.1.4
04E0 01 04		
05 00		NULL, len=0
03 81 81 00		BIT STRING, len=0x81, unused=0
4C 21 70 CC D6 3F EC 73		0x4C2170...
04F0 07 83 B2 78 3B C0 86 06 15 C1 97 ED 90 D7 3C B2		
0500 0F 6E DE 94 10 46 FD F1 1E 67 76 0D A3 DD 5D 92		
0510 DC 66 EC 4A 7A 61 03 AC E4 EF 00 7B 21 83 94 BE		
0520 AB A7 22 07 58 F8 0C 39 11 31 B3 A4 22 F5 BB 20		
0530 E2 BA C1 C2 3B 02 3A 26 95 C3 D0 2C 67 D3 F3 34		
0540 A3 C8 44 35 37 E9 E2 5E 5B ED 53 A8 07 07 79 D7		
0550 17 96 52 D3 50 14 5C C1 E1 41 88 CA A4 D6 17 84		
0560 46 49 AC B1 5C C8 3B 5A		

To clarify the relationship between the x.509 standard's definition of a certificate and an actual certificate, table A-19 repeats the ASN.1 definition. It then identifies the offset of each major ASN.1 component within the certificate.

Table A-19 Offsets of X.509 Certificate Components

Offset	ASN.1 Source	
0004	Certificate ::= SIGNED { SEQUENCE {	
0008	Version	[0] Version DEFAULT v1,
000D	serialNumber	CertificateSerialNumber,
001F	signature	AlgorithmIdentifier,
002E	issuer	Name,
00EB	validity	Validity,
010B	subject	Name,
0197	subjectPublicKeyInfo	SubjectPublicKeyInfo,
n.a.	issuerUniqueIdentifier	[1] IMPLICIT UniqueIdentifier OPTIONAL,
		-- if present, version must be v2 or v3
n.a.	subjectUniqueIdentifier	[2] IMPLICIT UniqueIdentifier OPTIONAL,
		-- if present, version must be v2 or v3
0238	extensions	[3] Extensions OPTIONAL
		-- If present, version must be v3 -- } }

The example certificate includes several OBJECT IDENTIFIER values. Table A-20 lists those that occur in the example certificate, along with a brief description of each. Some of the values in the actual certificate are privately administered, and thus their meanings are not publicly known.

Table A-20 OBJECT IDENTIFIER values in Example Certificate

OBJECT IDENTIFIER	Description	Offset(s)
1.2.840.113549.1.1.1	rsaEncryption	019C
1.2.840.113549.1.1.4	md5withRSAEncryption	0021, 04D7
1.3.6.1.4.1.311.10.3.3	Server Gated Cryptography	0497
2.5.4.3	commonName	017F
2.5.4.6	countryName	0112
2.5.4.7	localityName	0132
2.5.4.8	stateOrProvinceName	0121
2.5.4.10	organizationName	0035, 0145
2.5.4.11	organizationalUnitName	0056, 0071,

OBJECT IDENTIFIER	Description	Offset(s)
		00A4, 0160
2.5.29.3	certificatePolicies	024F
2.5.29.19	basicConstraints	0242
2.5.29.37	extKeyUsage	0483
2.16.840.1.113730.1.1	netscape-cert-type	0470
2.16.840.1.113730.4.1	International Step-Up	048C
2.16.840.1.113733.1.6.7	VeriSign unknown	04A5
2.16.840.1.113733.1.7.1.1	VeriSign certificatePolicy	0264
2.16.840.1.113733.1.7.1.1.1	VeriSign policy qualifier	0422
2.16.840.1.113733.1.7.1.1.2	VeriSign policy qualifier	0432

To conclude this section, table A-21 shows the logical content of the example certificate. It strips away the encoding information to focus on the essential elements of the certificate.

Table A-21 Contents of Example Certificate	
Version	X.509 version 3
Serial Number	0x3E29...
Algorithm Identifier	MD5 hash and RSA signing
Issuer:	
Organization	VeriSign Trust Network
Organizational Unit	VeriSign, Inc.
Organizational Unit	VeriSign International Server CA = Class 3
Organizational Unit	www.verisign.com/CPS ...
Validity:	
Not Before	1998-12-03 00:00.00 UTC
Not After	1999-12-11 23:59.59 UTC
Subject:	
Country	New Zealand
State or Province	Auckland

Locality	Auckland
Organization	ASB Bank Limited
Organizational Unit	Information Services
Common Name	www.asbbank.co.nz

Public Key Information:

Algorithm	RSA
Public Key	0x308188...

Extensions:

International Step-Up

Server Gated Cryptography

various VeriSign extensions

Algorithm Identifier	MD5 hash with RSA signing
Signature	0x4C2170...

Appendix B
SSL Security Checklist

The Secure Sockets Layer protocol has been in use for Web commerce for three years now, and under its new name of Transport Layer Security, the protocol is now in its fourth revision. Engineers now have quite a lot of experience with SSL and TLS implementations, much of which has helped to improve the security of the protocol through its revisions. Security specialists have also learned quite a lot about the relationship of SSL to other aspects of the systems that implement it. In fact, although there are no known security flaws in the SSL or TLS protocols themselves, other weaknesses in systems using SSL have been successfully exploited, at least in academic or research environments. This appendix considers those other weaknesses. It presents them in the form of an SSL security checklist, primarily for those readers who are designing or evaluating SSL implementations. Of course, the following list is not exhaustive, and new threats and attacks are likely to arise in the future. Readers should certainly stay up to date with security news and events to make sure that their implementations do not become vulnerable as new attacks are discovered.

This appendix considers security issues related to both the authentication and the encryption services of SSL. Each service receives its own section. In some cases, the distinction between the two is a bit artificial, as several issues have important effects for both services. For these, the appendix concludes with a section of general issues that are not easily characterized.

B.1 Authentication Issues

Authentication often seems to take a back seat to encryption in security discussions, especially in the trade press, where reports of cracking cryptographic algorithms receive prominent coverage. Ultimately, however, authentication is more critical to security. How secure, after all, is a system that establishes full-strength, encrypted communications with an attacker masquerading as the intended recipient? No amount of encryption can prevent an unsuspecting party sending an unauthenticated (or improperly authenticated) attacker the session keys. Although it may be tempting to overlook them, addressing authentication issues is vital to secure communication.

As this section makes clear, many of the issues of ssl authentication revolve around x.509 certificates. There are, however, some authentication issues specific to ssl that are independent of public key certificates.

B.1.1 Certificate Authority

A certificate authority (ca) signs all x.509 certificates, and any ssl implementation must decide whether it can trust the ca of its communicating peer. Typically, implementations compare the peer's ca with an internal list of authorities that the implementation "knows" to be trustworthy. With this approach, it is important that the implementation use the public key from its internal store to verify the certificate, rather than the public key from the ca certificate provided by the peer. Attackers can construct fake ca certificates that are identical to real certificates in all areas except the public key, substituting a public key corresponding to the attacker's private key. Only by retrieving ca public keys from its internal store would an implementation prevent such an attack.

If an implementation does decide to keep an internal list of trusted certificate authorities, it must carefully consider how, if at all, it will allow users to update that list. For short-lived implementations, such updates may not be needed. In general, however, users will need a way to revise the set of trusted authorities. Even ca certificates, for example, expire eventually.

B.1.2   Certificate Signature

This point may seem obvious, but it can be easy to overlook: an SSL implementation must validate all certificates it receives by verifying the CA signature within them.

B.1.3   Certificate Validity Times

All SSL implementations should also check the validity period for all certificates. The validity period includes both a "not before" and a "not after" time; both should be verified. As an additional twist, note that the ASN.1 object used for time in X.509 certificates (the UTCTime string) only provides two decimal digits for the year. All appropriate Y2K concerns apply.

B.1.4   Certificate Revocation Status

Implementations that operate in environments that support certificate revocation should check the revocation status of any certificate before accepting it. Unfortunately, not all environments effectively support certificate revocation. The Web, for example, does not have a widely deployed mechanism for disseminating certificate revocation lists. In such cases, an implementation may want to provide users an alternative, perhaps by permitting the manual import of certificate revocation lists.

B.1.5   Certificate Subject

Perhaps it should go without saying, but an implementation must not only ensure that a certificate is valid; the implementation must also make sure that it certifies the right party. An attacker may well be able to get a perfectly valid certificate from a legitimate certificate authority. That certificate will simply be a certificate for the attacker. An implementation that tries to communicate with confidant.com, and instead receives a certificate for evilhacker.com, had better notice the discrepancy, no matter how valid the certificate.

Exactly how an implementation verifies that the certificate is for the intended subject depends on the policies of the certificate authority. VeriSign Class 3 certificates, for example, place the host name of the certified Web site in the commonName field of the certificate's subject. Both Netscape Navigator and Internet Explorer check this field against the host name that the user enters in the URL (or that appears in the referring link).

B.1.6 Diffie-Hellman Trapdoors

When SSL implementations use ephemeral Diffie-Hellman key exchange, the server specifies a full set of Diffie-Hellman parameters. There are, however, legitimate disagreements about what constitutes sufficiently secure Diffie-Hellman parameters.[1] Clients that support ephemeral Diffie-Hellman key exchange should check the parameters they receive from the server. They should ensure that the server has chosen values that the client believes will provide adequate security.

B.1.7 Algorithm Rollback

With a ServerKeyExchange message, an SSL server sends the client public key information the client needs to encrypt the premaster secret for the server. This key information is signed by the server using the private key corresponding to the public key in the server's Certificate message. The public key algorithm the client is to use, however, is not specified explicitly in the ServerKeyExchange message, so that information is not signed by the server. This could make the SSL protocol vulnerable to an *algorithm rollback attack*.

In an algorithm rollback attack, the attacker forces the two parties to have different opinions as to which public key algorithm is to be used

---

[1] For example, in *Network Security* (Prentice-Hall, 1995), C. Kaufman, R. Perlman, and M. Speciner suggest that Diffie-Hellman prime numbers should have a special property that makes them *strong primes*. Bruse Schneier, on the other hand, argues in *Applied Cryptography* (John Wiley & Sons, 1996) that strong primes do not improve the security.

to sign the premaster secret. The client, for example, might be fooled into believing that RSA encryption is appropriate, while the server expects Diffie-Hellman. David Wagner and Bruce Schneier show[2] how this scenario leads to a complete breakdown of all cryptographic protection. The attacker is able to read all information for the session or to forge fake data in the name of either party.

To protect against this algorithm rollback attack, SSL client implementations should verify the length and number of parameters in any ServerKeyExchange message. As figures 4-10 and 4-11 indicated, RSA encryption requires only two parameters, while Diffie-Hellman uses three. If, in any received message, the lengths of the individual parameters and the signed hash values do not add up to the correct length of the whole message, then the client should reject the session and generate an appropriate alert.

B.1.8 Dropped ChangeCipherSpec Messages

The SSL protocol does not include ChangeCipherSpec messages in the handshake authentication code that Finished messages carry. ChangeCipherSpec messages are omitted because SSL does not consider them to be Handshake protocol messages. (Recall that ChangeCipherSpec messages belong to their own separate SSL subprotocol.) This omission does leave SSL implementations vulnerable to a particular attack when the parties use authentication-only (i.e., no encryption) sessions.

To take advantage of this vulnerability, the attacker simply deletes the ChangeCipherSpec messages from the communication stream. Both parties will receive an apparently valid Finished message and begin transferring application data, without ever activating the cipher suite they have negotiated. (This attack is not feasible when the session uses encryption. In that case, the party sending a Finished message will encrypt it, while the party receiving the Finished message,

---

[2] In "Analysis of the SSL 3.0 Protocol" (see the References section); this paper was the first to publish a description of this attack.

not having seen the missing ChangeCipherSpec message, will expect it unencrypted.)

Fortunately, combating this attack is very straightforward. An SSL implementation should not accept a Finished message unless it has also received a ChangeCipherSpec message.

B.2 Encryption Issues

Aside from the contentious legal issues that can limit the effectiveness of any security implementation, SSL is very effective in protecting the confidentiality of information. There are a few minor points to consider, however. This section reviews the importance of encryption key size, and examines two other concerns about SSL encryption: a potential traffic analysis weakness and an attack first identified by Daniel Bleichenbacher.

B.2.1 Encryption Key Size

One important issue that arises repeatedly is the strength of the encryption that SSL offers. That strength depends most directly on the size of the keys used by the symmetric encryption algorithms, such as RC4 and DES. In theory, developers could create SSL implementations that only used sufficiently large key sizes, and such implementations would be practically unbreakable. Some governments, however, place restrictions on the use or export of cryptography. The laws and regulations of the United States (home to many key SSL developers) forced the creation of the "export strength" SSL cipher suites, which, because of their limited key size, are much weaker than the protocol allows. Indeed, sessions encrypted using these cipher suites were successfully attacked as early as 1995,[3] and most security professionals today consider the SSL export strength cipher suites to offer only

---

[3] Reported in "Netscape Security Encryption is Cracked—Breach Spurs Concern for Commerce on Internet," *San Jose Mercury News*, 17 August 1995. Information is also available at http://pauillac.inria.fr/~doligez/ssl/.

marginal security. The situation did not improve significantly when the U.S. government relaxed its regulations to allow export of stronger cryptography. The stronger 56-bit encryption was compromised in 1998.[4]

Secure Socket Layer implementations should carefully evaluate the value of the information they will protect and weigh that against the strength of the security they can offer. If the information is sufficiently valuable, and if the implementation would be subject to laws or regulations that would restrict its encryption strength, compromise solutions might be the most viable. Netscape's International Step-Up and Microsoft's Server Gated Cryptography are both examples of how stronger security is possible in the context of laws and regulations.

B.2.2 Traffic Analysis

Attackers may learn a lot about a target just by observing the traffic to and from that target, even if they cannot actually decrypt the information. *Traffic analysis*, as such attacks are known, is difficult to defend against in an open environment such as the Internet. (Indeed, many Web sites like to publicize the amount and type of traffic they receive.) In any environment, however, the SSL protocol itself introduces an additional traffic analysis vulnerability. When SSL uses a stream cipher for encryption, the size of the encrypted messages can reveal the size of the unencrypted data; the attacker needs only to subtract the size of the message authentication code. Bennet Yee[5] has noted how this weakness could allow an attacker to discover some information about an encrypted session, including, for example, which specific Web pages were retrieved by a user (though not the contents of those pages). This weakness is not present if block encryption ciphers are used, since the padding they introduce effectively hides the exact size of the plaintext data. If the application warrants it, SSL im-

---

[4] See *Cracking DES: Secrets of Encryption Research, Wiretap Politics & Chip Design* by the Electronic Frontier Foundation, published by O'Reilly & Associates in 1998.
[5] As reported in Wagner and Schneier.

plementations may choose to support only block encryption cipher suites in order to protect against this traffic analysis attack.

B.2.3 The Bleichenbacher Attack

In 1998, Daniel Bleichenbacher, a researcher at Lucent's Bell Laboratories, reported a specific active attack against security protocols that use RSA encryption, including the SSL protocol.[6] The attack takes advantage of the way the RSA encryption algorithm encodes data before encrypting it. The encoded data (which SSL uses as a symmetric encryption key) always begins with the two bytes 00 and 02. Table B-1 shows how an attacker can exploit this characteristic.

Table B-1 The Bleichenbacher Attack

Step	Action
1	The attacker carefully constructs many artificial ciphertext blocks and sends them to the target. (Since the attacker doesn't know the target's private key, the attacker won't know how these ciphertext blocks will be decrypted. At this point, that is not important, though.)
2	The target receives the artificial ciphertext blocks and decrypts them.
a	For most of the blocks, the resulting "plaintext" will not conform to the RSA encoding format. (It won't begin with the bytes 00 and 02.) In those cases, the target generates an error or perhaps ignores the communication.
b	Occasionally a ciphertext block will happen to decrypt into plaintext that begins with the magic 00 and 02 bytes. In those cases, the target treats the decryption as successful and attempts to use the rest of the "plaintext" for its intended purpose. (Since the plaintext is effectively just random data, the target is likely to eventually realize that something is wrong with its data. By that time, however, it may be too late.)

---

[6] Details can be found in Bleichenbacher's paper "Chosen Ciphertext Attacks against Protocols Based on RSA Encryption Standard PKCS #1" in *Advances in Cryptology—Crypto'98*, LNCS vol. 1462, pp. 1–12, 1998, published by Springer-Verlag. The attack is also described in RSA Laboratories' Bulletin Number 7 (26 June 1998), available at this writing from the RSA Web site at http://www.rsasecurity.com/rsalabs/bulletins/.

Step	Action
3	The attacker observes the target's reaction to each artificial ciphertext block, noting which blocks cause response 2a and which cause response 2b.
4	By carefully choosing its artificial ciphertext blocks, and by refining those choices as the attack progresses, the attacker can use sophisticated mathematical analyses to decipher a related ciphertext block, perhaps one that was actually sent to the target as part of legitimate communications.

In practice, Bleichenbacher's strategy does have a significant limitation. The number of artificial ciphertext blocks it requires can be quite large. For a 1024-bit RSA modulus (the standard key size for Web security not subject to U.S. export restrictions), the attacker must generate about 2^{20} (just over 1 million) different artificial ciphertext blocks. This limitation will likely warn any reasonably vigilant target that an attack may be under way.

In addition, there are several other steps that SSL implementations can take to reduce their exposure to this attack. One step is to rigorously check the decrypted plaintext before accepting it as a valid decryption. In the case of received ClientKeyExchange messages, implementations should ensure that the premaster secret is the correct size (48 bytes) and that the first 2 bytes are the SSL version number, in addition to verifying the presence of the 00 and 02 bytes. Those steps alone will increase the number of artificial ciphertext blocks the attack requires from 2^{20} to more than 2^{40} (about 20 million).

Another design principle that can thwart this attack is to be very parsimonious in sending error responses. Ideally, an SSL implementation would behave consistently, whether it was unable to decrypt a ClientKeyExchange message or it decrypted successfully but found the resulting plaintext to be invalid. One possible implementation is to ignore the fact that decrypted ClientKeyExchange data does not conform to the RSA encoding format. (In other words, it does not begin with 00 02.) A convenient way to achieve this may be to replace any such invalid data with *random* data that does conform. The server will then detect and respond to the error just as if the invalid data had been appropriately formatted.

Finally, please note that the symmetric encryption key that is encrypted by the RSA algorithm is the only information at risk from this attack. The attack does not compromise any RSA private keys.

B.3 General Issues

A few important issues do not easily fit the categories of either authentication or encryption. This section discusses those issues, including the problems of RSA key size, version rollback attacks, premature closures, session ID values, random number generation, and random number seeding.

B.3.1 RSA Key Size

The majority of SSL implementations today use the RSA encryption algorithm for digital signatures and public key encryption. The strength of the RSA algorithm depends directly on the size of the RSA public key. Longer keys yield more secure implementations. As the availability of computing power has increased and its cost has decreased, key sizes that were once thought adequately secure are now susceptible to brute-force attacks. While the author was preparing this manuscript, a team of researchers announced that they had successfully cracked an RSA key of 512 bits,[7] the same key size that (due to U.S. export restrictions) is commonly used to secure most Web transactions. The team used several hundred computers full-time for seven months, so there may not be an immediate practical threat to existing systems, but RSA Laboratories recommends 768 bits as the minimum acceptable key size for the RSA algorithm.

It is important to understand that a weakness or compromise of the RSA algorithm may be far more severe than one in symmetric encryp-

---

[7] See http://www.rsasecurity.com/rsalabs/factoring/rsa155.html.

tion algorithms such as RC4 or DES. Symmetric algorithms provide the encryption for individual SSL sessions. If a particular symmetric encryption key is compromised, only information from the session that used the key is exposed. The RSA public key algorithm, however, is used both to authenticate parties and to securely exchange all session keys. If a particular RSA private key is compromised, then the owner of that key is vulnerable to impersonation, and the information from *all* SSL sessions with that party may be exposed.

B.3.2 Version Rollback Attacks

Secure Sockets Layer version 3.0 introduced several improvements to version 2.0, including those that increased the security of the protocol. It is important, therefore, that two parties that are capable of using version 3.0 actually do so, instead of falling back to the less secure version 2.0. As section 5.1.1 indicated, the SSL specification outlines a very specific approach to protect against attacks that force a version rollback. There is, however, one area that the specification does not address: resumption of prior sessions. A cursory SSL implementation might allow a session that had previously been established using version 3.0 to be resumed using version 2.0. Such an implementation would comply with the SSL standard. Careful implementations, though, should not allow this behavior. If a session is established using SSL version 3.0, then the implementation should ensure that all attempts to resume the session also use SSL version 3.0.

B.3.3 Premature Closure

Another general security issue is the threat of truncation attacks due to the premature closure of an SSL session. If an attacker can delete protocol messages in transit, that attacker could create a scenario in which one or both of the communicating parties only receive partial information. If the missing information is vital to the communications, the attacker will have compromised the overall security of the exchange. As section 3.4 discussed, the SSL protocol defines the ClosureAlert message to protect against this type of attack. (Although the ClosureAlert can't prevent the attack, the absence of a ClosureAlert message at least alerts the parties to the potential problem.) Unfortunately, not all environments can rely on the ClosureAlert. Web browsing users, for example, may simply turn off their personal computer after completing a transaction, before that computer has a chance to send a ClosureAlert message. More thorough protection requires that applications using SSL security be sensitive to the possibility of premature closures. Web servers that support the HyperText Transfer Protocol (HTTP), for example, include a Content-Length field with each page they send to a client. Clients should verify that the amount of data they receive is consistent with this field's value.

B.3.4 SessionID Values

The SSL specification gives servers complete flexibility to choose particular SessionID values. In making this choice, server implementation should be careful not to include any critical security information. SessionID values are transferred in ClientHello and ServerHello messages before any encryption is active. Their values, therefore, are completely exposed to any potential attacker.

B.3.5 Random Number Generation

Random numbers are critical to the operation of the Secure Sockets Layer protocol. The random numbers exchanged in ClientHello and ServerHello messages ultimately determine the encryption key for the session. Random numbers, however, present an interesting challenge to computer systems; software cannot do anything truly randomly. Instead, software implementations typically rely on algorithms known as pseudorandom number generators. These algorithms simulate true randomness with complex mathematical calculations.

There are two problems with pseudorandom number generators that should concern SSL and other security implementations. The first problem is the effectiveness of the algorithms themselves. Most software libraries generate pseudorandom numbers using a *linear congruential generator* algorithm. Although such algorithms can be effective pseudorandom number generators, they can also be quite ineffective. Furthermore, many developers seek to improve on the basic algorithm in ways that can, in fact, be quite disastrous. Press, Teukolsky, Vetterling, and Flannery report on one widely used pseudorandom number generator that, in an extreme case, effectively generated only 11 distinct random values.[8]

A more serious problem with linear congruential generators is that they are sequential, and completely predictable. If you know the parameters of the algorithm and one specific value, it is easy to predict all future values that the algorithm will generate. Predictable random numbers are a serious problem for any security protocol, as they allow attackers to plan and prepare well into the future, waiting, perhaps, for a single, compromised value to appear. Implementations of SSL, therefore, should be careful not to use common pseudorandom number generator libraries. Fortunately, standard cryptography algorithms, including both encryption and hash algorithms, can be modified to provide effective random numbers.[9]

B.3.6   Random Number Seeding

Regardless of the algorithm implementations used to generate random numbers, implementations typically must provide that algorithm with an initial starting point, or *seed*. For applications other than security, the primary requirement for this seed is that it be different each time it is generated. That ensures, for example, that a computer game does not act the same at each playing. That has led many developers to use some form of the time of day as the seed. For security applications, however, random seeds not only must be different, they must also be unpredictable. The time of day is rarely unpredictable. Indeed, Matthew Schmid[10] reports a successful attack

---

[8] In the second edition of *Numerical Recipes in C: The Art of Scientific Computing* (Cambridge University Press, 1992), p. 277. Chapter 7 includes a thorough (and sobering) discussion of random number generation.

[9] More information is available from RSA Laboratories' Bulletins Number 1 (22 January 1996) and Number 8 (3 September 1998), available as of this writing at http://www.rsasecurity.com/rsalabs/bulletins/.

[10] In a posting to the Risks Forum at http://catless.ncl.ac.uk/Risks/20.56.html.

against several online gambling sites that rely on flawed software for their online poker games. The software used the time of day to seed its random number generator and, as a result, attackers were able to successfully predict the cards in every player's hand. Although not strictly ssl-related, the lesson is clear: using the time of day for random seeds is totally unacceptable for ssl implementations.[11]

---

[11] Bulletins from rsa Laboratories, in this case Numbers 1 (22 January 1996) and 3 (25 January 1996), offer detailed advice on seeding random number generators. See http://www.rsasecurity.com/rsalabs/bulletins/.

References

The following sources have more detailed information on many topics in this text. Individual references, with commentary, are grouped by protocol standards, certificate formats, cryptographic algorithms, and SSL implementations.

Protocol Standards

The official specification for the Secure Sockets Layer Protocol (version 3.0) is available in several formats from the Netscape Web site at http://www.netscape.com/eng/ssl3/.

> Alan O. Freier, Philip Karlton, and Paul C. Kocher. *The SSL Protocol Version 3.0.* Netscape Communications Corporation. 4 March 1996.

Please note that some of the formats include errata to the original specification. The errata itself are also available from the same site.

> *SSL 3.0 Errata.* 26 August 1996.

The Transport Layer Security specification is a proposed standard of the Internet Engineering Task Force (IETF). IETF documents may be found from the organization's Web site at http://www.ietf.org.

> T. Dierks and C. Allen. *The TLS Protocol Version 1.0* [RFC 2246]. The Internet Engineering Task Force, January 1999.

Additional information on TLS, including other related documents, meeting minutes, and mailing list archives, is available on the IETF Web site at http://www.ietf.org/html.charters/tls-charter.html.

Formal, detailed documents on Netscape's International Step-Up or Microsoft's Server Gated Cryptography are not available as of this writing; however, each company's Web site does include some information. The information Netscape makes available may be found at http://developer.netscape.com/tech/security/stepup/, while Microsoft describes SGC at http://www.microsoft.com/security/tech/sgc/. In addition, VeriSign has some information on both enhancements in the description of its Global Site ID available from its home page at http://www.verisign.com.

Finally, the definitive security analysis of the Secure Sockets Layer protocol is that of David Wagner and Bruce Schneier. Their paper is available at http://www.counterpane.com/ssl.html.

> David Wagner and Bruce Schneier. "Analysis of the SSL 3.0 Protocol," *The Second USENIX Workshop on Electronic Commerce Proceedings*, USENIX Press, November 1996, pp. 29–40.

Certificate Formats

The X.509 specifications for public key certificates are available, for a fee, from the International Telecommunications Union. These can be purchased directly from the ITU Web site at www.itu.ch. (Yes, the ITU does use SSL to secure this electronic commerce!). The X.509 standard itself contains the definition of a certificate; X.680 through X.683 define the Abstract Syntax Notation One, and X.690 defines the distinguished encoding rules for encoding ASN.1. Note that many of the ITU specifications have amendments and corrections (which the ITU calls *corrigenda*) which are also available from the ITU.

> *Recommendation X.509 (08/97) - Information technology - Open Systems Interconnection - The Directory: Authentication framework.* The International Telecommunications Union, August 1997.

> *Recommendation X.680 (12/97) - Information technology - Abstract Syntax Notation One (ASN.1): Specification of basic notation.* The International Telecommunications Union, December 1997.

> *Recommendation X.681 (12/97) - Information technology - Abstract Syntax Notation One (ASN.1): Information object specification.*

The International Telecommunications Union, December 1997.

Recommendation X.682 (12/97) - Information technology - Abstract Syntax Notation One (ASN.1): Constraint specification. The International Telecommunications Union, December 1997.

Recommendation X.683 (12/97) - Information technology - Abstract Syntax Notation One (ASN.1): Parameterization of ASN.1 specifications. The International Telecommunications Union, December 1997.

Recommendation X.690 (12/97) - Information technology - ASN.1 encoding rules; Specification of Basic Encoding Rules (BER), Canonical Encoding Rules (CER) and Distinguished Encoding Rules (DER). The International Telecommunications Union, December 1997.

Cryptographic Algorithms

Three cryptographic algorithms of particular importance to many SSL implementations are the MD5 and SHA hash algorithms and the RSA public key encryption (and digital signature) algorithm. Descriptions of these algorithms may be found in the following references.

National Institute of Standards and Technology. "Secure Hash Standard [NIST FIPS PUB 180-1]." U.S. Department of Commerce. Work in progress, May 31, 1994.

R. Rivest. *The MD5 Message-Digest Algorithm* [RFC 1321]. Internet Engineering Task Force, April 1992.

R. Rivest, A. Shamir, and L. Adleman. "A Method for Obtaining Digital Signatures and Public-Key Cryptosystems." *Communications of the ACM*, 21(2), pp. 120–126, February 1978.

In addition, the following two books cover these cryptographic algorithms, as well as many others. Schneier's work is thorough and comprehensive; the Kaufman et al. text is more introductory in na-

ture, with particular emphasis on security for network communications.

C. Kaufman, R. Perlman, and M. Speciner. *Network Security: Private Communications in a Public World.* Prentice Hall, 1995.

Bruce Schneier. *Applied Cryptography Second Edition: Protocols, Algorithms, and Source Code in C.* John Wiley and Sons, Inc., 1996.

SSL Implementations

In addition to reference text, some readers may appreciate actual
software source code implementations of the SSL protocol. Although
many vendors offer commercial software that implements SSL, two
source code implementations are available for free. Netscape provides
a reference implementation of SSL (currently restricted to the United
States). As of this writing, information is available from Netscape at
http://www.netscape.com/products/security/ssl/reference.html.   Ad-
ditionally, the OpenSSL Project is a collaborative effort to develop
an SSL toolkit available as open source software. The project's home
page is http://www.openssl.org/.

Glossary

Abstract Syntax Notation One (ASN.1). A language for describing data and data objects, used to define x.509 public key certificates.

Active Attack. An attack against a secure communications session in which the attacker creates and sends his or her own messages or modifies legitimate messages in transit between the communicating parties.

Alert Description. A single-byte value that identifies the type of SSL alert.

Alert Message. An SSL message that indicates that the sender has detected an error condition.

Alert Protocol. A component of the SSL protocol that defines the format of Alert messages.

Alteration. An attack in which the attacker attempts to modify information without being detected.

Asymmetric Encryption. The technical term for public key encryption in which two different keys are used for encryption and decryption; one of the keys can be revealed publicly without compromising security.

Asymmetric Key Cryptography. Cryptography based on asymmetric encryption; depending on the particular algorithms employed, asymmetric key cryptography can provide encryption/decryption or digital signature services.

Attack. An attempt to compromise or defeat the security of a communications session.

Authentication. A security service that validates the identity of a communicating party.

BIT STRING. An ASN.1 primitive object that represents an arbitrary number of bits.

Block Cipher. A cipher that encrypts and decrypts data only in fixed-size blocks.

BOOLEAN. An ASN.1 primitive object that represents a value that can only be true or false.

Certificate. A public key certificate, digital information that identifies a subject and that subject's public key and is digitally signed by an authority that certifies the information it contains.

Certificate Authority (CA). An organization that issues certificates and vouches for the identities of the subjects of those certificates; also known as an issuer.

Certificate Chain. A series of certificates including a subject's certificate, the certificate for the root authority, and any intermediate certificate authorities; it establishes a chain of trust from the subject all the way to the root.

Certificate Message. An SSL handshake message that carries a certificate chain.

CertificateRequest Message. An SSL handshake message that the server sends to ask the client to authenticate its identity.

Certificate Type. Part of an SSL CertificateRequest message that indicates the digital signature and public key algorithms that the sender will accept.

CertificateVerify Message. An SSL handshake message that the client sends to verify that it possesses the private key corresponding to its certificate; the client digitally signs part of the message using that private key.

ChangeCipherSpec Message. An SSL message that activates the negotiated security parameters; those parameters will be in effect for the next message that the sender transmits.

ChangeCipherSpec Protocol. The SSL protocol for Change-CipherSpec messages.

CHOICE. An ASN.1 construction that specifies that exactly one of the indicated objects may be present.

Cipher. An algorithm that encrypts and decrypts information.

Cipher Suite. A cipher algorithm and the parameters necessary to specify its use (e.g., size of keys.)

Ciphertext. Information that has been encrypted using a cipher.

Class (of a tag). The context under which an ASN.1 tag is defined: universal, application-specific, private, and context-specific.

Client. The party that initiates communications; clients communicate with servers.

ClientHello Message. An SSL handshake message that the client sends to propose cipher suites for the communication.

ClientKeyExchange Message. An SSL message that the client sends to give the server information needed to construct key material for the communication.

Compression Method. A particular data compression algorithm and parameters needed to specify its use.

Confidentiality. A security service that protects information from being correctly interpreted by parties other than those participating in the communication.

Cryptanalysis. The science concentrating on the study of methods and techniques to defeat cryptography.

Cryptography. The science concentrating on the study of methods and techniques to provide security by mathematical manipulation of information.

Cryptology. The science encompassing both cryptography and cryptanalysis.

Data Encryption Standard (DES). A symmetric encryption algorithm published by the National Institutes of Science and

Technology as a United States standard; DES is a block cipher operating on 56-bit blocks.

Decipher. To decrypt encrypted information.

Decryption. The complement of encryption, recovering the original information from encrypted data.

Diffie-Hellman. A key exchange algorithm developed by W. Diffie and M.E. Hellman; first published in 1976.

Digest Function. A cryptographic function that creates a digital summary of information so that, if the information is altered, the summary (known as a hash) will also change; also known as a hash function.

Digital Signature. The result of encrypting information with the private key of a public/private key pair; the public key can be used to successfully decrypt the signature, proving that only someone possessing the private key could have created it.

Digital Signature Algorithm (DSA). An asymmetric encryption algorithm published as a U.S. standard by the National Institutes of Science and Technology; DSA can only be used to sign data.

Distinguished Encoding Rules (DER). A process for unambiguously converting an object specified in ASN.1 into binary values for storage or transmission on a network.

Distinguished Name. The identity of a subject or issuer specified according to a hierarchy of objects defined by the ITU.

Eavesdropping. An attack against the security of a communication in which the attacker attempts to "overhear" the communication.

Encipher. To encrypt information by applying a cipher algorithm; the result is unintelligible, and the original information can only be recovered by someone who can decipher the result.

Encryption. The process of applying a cipher algorithm to information, resulting in data that is unintelligible to anyone who does not have sufficient information to reverse the encryption.

Ephemeral Diffie-Hellman. Diffie-Hellman key exchange in which the necessary parameters are created just for a single communications session.

Explicit Diffie-Hellman. Diffie-Hellman key exchange in which some of the parameters are established in advance.

Explicit Tag. A type of ASN.1 tag in which the tag value for the tagged object's type is also included in the encoding.

Exportable. Said of security products that may be easily licensed for export from the United States, generally those with encryption algorithms that only use limited key sizes.

File Transfer Protocol (FTP). An Internet application protocol for transferring files among computer systems; SSL can provide security for FTP communications.

Finished Message. An SSL handshake message that indicates the sender has completed security negotiations.

Forgery. An attack against secure communications in which the attacker tries to create data that appears to come from one of the communicating parties.

Fortezza. A classified encryption and key exchange algorithm developed by the U.S. government, the details of which are not publicly known.

Global Secure ID. The brand name for Web security certificates, issued by VeriSign, that support International Step-Up and Server Gated Cryptography.

Handshake Protocol. A component protocol of SSL responsible for negotiating security parameters.

Hash Function. A cryptographic function that creates a digital summary of information so that, if the information is altered, the summary (known as a hash) will also change; also known as a digest function.

Hashed MAC. A standard approach to using hash algorithms to create secure message authentication codes.

HelloRequest Message. An SSL handshake message with which the server requests that a client restart negotiations.

HyperText Transfer Protocol (HTTP). The application protocol for Web browsing; SSL can add security to HTTP applications.

IA5String. An ASN.1 primitive object representing a character string from the ASCII character set.

Implicit Tag. A type of ASN.1 tag in which the tag value for the tagged object's type is not included in the encoding.

Initialization Vector (IV). Random data that serves as the initial input to an encryption algorithm so that the algorithm may build up to full strength before it encrypts actual data.

INTEGER. An ASN.1 object that represents a whole number.

International Step-Up. Developed by Netscape; an addition to normal SSL procedures that allows servers to determine whether a client can exercise latent security services that are otherwise not permitted by U.S. export laws; similar (but not identical) to Server Gated Cryptography.

International Telecommunications Union (ITU). An international standards body responsible for telecommunications protocols; the ITU publishes the X.509 standards for public key certificates.

Internet Engineering Task Force (IETF). An international standards body responsible for Internet protocols; the IETF publishes the Transport Layer Security specifications.

Internet Protocol (IP). The core network protocol for the Internet; IP is responsible for routing messages from their source to their destination.

IP Security Protocol (IPSEC). Enhancements to the Internet Protocol that allow it to provide security services.

Issuer. An organization that issues certificates and vouches for the identities of the subjects of those certificates; also known as a certificate authority.

Kerberos. A network security protocol designed to provide authorization and access control services.

Key. Information needed to encrypt or decrypt data; to preserve security, symmetric encryption algorithms must protect the confidentiality of all keys, while asymmetric encryption algorithms need only protect private keys.

Key Exchange Algorithm. An algorithm that allows two parties to agree on a secret key without actually transferring the key value across an insecure channel; the best known example is the Diffie-Hellman key exchange.

Key Management. The procedures for creating and distributing cryptographic keys.

MAC Read Secret. A secret value input to a message authentication code algorithm for verifying the integrity of received data; one party's MAC write secret is the other party's MAC read secret.

MAC Write Secret. A secret value input to a message authentication code algorithm to generate message authentication codes for data that is to be transmitted; one party's MAC write secret is the other party's MAC read secret.

Man-in-the-Middle Attack. An attack against secure communications in which the attacker interposes itself between the communicating parties, relaying information between them; the attacker can seek either to read the secured data or to modify it.

Masquerade. An attack against secure communications in which the attacker attempts to assume the identity of one of the communicating parties.

Master Secret. The value created as the result of SSL security negotiations, from which all secret key material is derived.

Message Authentication Code (MAC). An algorithm that uses cryptographic technology to create a digital summary of information so that, if the information is altered, the summary (known as a hash) will also change.

Message Digest 5 (MD5). A digest function designed by Ron Rivest and used extensively by SSL.

Message Integrity. A security service that allows detection of any alteration of protected data.

Net News Transfer Protocol (NNTP). An Internet application for transfer of news and news group information; NNTP can be secured with SSL.

Non-repudiation. A security service that prevents a party from falsely denying that it was the source of data that it did indeed create.

NULL. An ASN.1 primitive object that represents no information.

OBJECT IDENTIFIER. An ASN.1 primitive type that represents objects in an internationally administered registry of values.

OCTET STRING. An ASN.1 primitive type representing an arbitrary array of bytes.

Padding. Extra data added to information to force a specific block size.

Passive Attack. An attack against secure communications in which the attacker merely observes and monitors the communicating parties without actively participating in the communications.

Plaintext. Information in its unencrypted (and vulnerable) form before encryption or after decryption.

Premaster Secret. An intermediate value SSL implementation uses in the process of calculating key material for a session; the client usually creates the premaster secret from random data and sends it to the server in a ClientKeyExchange message.

PrintableString. An ASN.1 primitive type that represents an array of characters, all of which have textual representations.

Private Communication Technology (PCT). A technology developed by Microsoft that borrows from and improves upon SSL version 2.0; many of its features were incorporated into SSL version 3.0.

Private Key. One of the keys used in asymmetric cryptography; it cannot be publicly revealed without compromising security, but only one party to a communication needs to know its value.

Pseudorandom Function (PRF). An algorithm TLS defines to generate random numbers for use in key material message integrity.

Pseudorandom Number. A number generated by a computer that has all the properties of a true random number.

Public Key. One of the keys used in asymmetric cryptography; it can be publicly revealed without compromising security.

Public Key Certificate. Digital information that identifies a subject and that subject's public key and that is digitally signed by an authority that certifies the information it contains.

Public Key Cryptography. Cryptography based on asymmetric encryption in which two different keys are used for encryption and decryption; one of the keys can be revealed publicly without compromising the other key.

Record Layer. The component of the SSL protocol responsible for formatting and framing all SSL messages.

Rivest Cipher 2 (RC2). A block cipher developed by Ron Rivest.

Rivest Cipher 4 (RC4). A stream cipher developed by Ron Rivest.

Rivest Shamir Adleman (RSA). An asymmetric encryption algorithm named after its three developers; RSA supports both encryption and digital signatures.

Secret Key. A key used in symmetric encryption algorithms and other cryptographic functions in which both parties must know the same key information.

Secret Key Cryptography. Cryptography based on symmetric encryption in which both parties must possess the same key information.

Secure Hash Algorithm (SHA). A hash algorithm published as a U.S. standard by the National Institutes of Science and Technology.

Secure HyperText Transfer Protocol (S-HTTP). An addition to the HyperText Transfer Protocol application that provides security services.

Secure Sockets Layer (SSL). A separate network security protocol developed by Netscape and widely deployed for securing Web transactions.

SEQUENCE. An ASN.1 construction that represents an ordered collection of more primitive objects.

SEQUENCE OF. An ASN.1 construction representing a collection of multiple instances of a single, more primitive object, in which the order of the instances is important.

Server. The party in a communication that receives and responds to requests initiated by the other party.

Server Gated Cryptography (SGC). Developed by Microsoft, an addition to normal SSL procedures that allows servers to determine whether a client can exercise latent security services that are otherwise not permitted by U.S. export laws; similar (but not identical) to International Step-Up.

ServerHello Message. An SSL handshake message in which the server identifies the security parameters that will be used for the session.

ServerHelloDone Message. An SSL handshake message that the server sends to indicate it has concluded its part of the handshake negotiations.

ServerKeyExchange Message. An SSL handshake message in which the server sends public key information that the client should use to encrypt the premaster secret.

SessionID. The value SSL servers assign to a particular session so that it may be resumed at a later point with full renegotiation.

SET. An ASN.1 construction that represents an unordered collection of more primitive objects.

SET OF. An ASN.1 construction that represents a collection of multiple instances of a single, more primitive object, in which the order of the instances is not important.

Severity Level. A component of an SSL alert message that indicates whether the alert condition is fatal or merely a warning.

Signature. The encryption of information with a private key; anyone possessing the corresponding public key can verify that the private key was used, but only a party with the private key can create the signature.

Stream Cipher. A cipher that can encrypt and decrypt arbitrary amounts of data, in contrast to block ciphers.

Subject. The party who possesses a private key and whose identity is certified by a public key certificate.

Symmetric Encryption. The technical term for secret key encryption in which encryption and decryption require the same key information.

Symmetric Key Cryptography. Cryptography based on symmetric encryption; depending on the particular algorithms employed, symmetric key cryptography can provide encryption/decryption and message integrity services.

Tag. A value associated with an ASN.1 object that allows that particular object to be unambiguously identified in encoded data.

TeletexString. An ASN.1 primitive type representing character strings limited to Teletex characters.

Traffic Analysis. A passive attack against secure communications in which the attacker seeks to compromise security merely by observing the patterns and volume of traffic between the parties, without knowing the contents of the communication.

Transmission Control Protocol (TCP). A core protocol of the Internet that ensures the reliable transmission of data from source to destination.

Transport Layer Security (TLS). The IETF standard version of the Secure Sockets Layer protocol.

UTCTime. An ASN.1 primitive object that represents time according the universal standard (formerly known as Greenwich Mean Time).

X.509. An ITU standard for public key certificates.

Index

About the CD-ROM

The CD-ROM includes electronic editions of the full text of this book. Due to memory constraints, illustrations in the printed book are not available in all formats; however, key illustrations are recreated in the electronic editions as tables. System requirements for each format are listed below.

PalmOS

- Handheld computer such as the Handspring Visor, 3Com PalmPilot Pro, Palm III, Palm IIIe, Palm IIIx, Palm V, Palm Vx, Palm VII, or IBM WorkPad running PalmOS Version 2.0 or later.

- At least 220K of free memory.

Windows CE

- Windows CE computer (Handheld, Palm, or Handheld Pro) running Windows CE Version 2.0 or later.

- At least 260K of free storage space.

- At least 256K of free program space.

Other Platforms

- Adobe Acrobat Reader version 3.0 or later, available for download at http://www.adobe.com.